Guitar Secrets Revealed

Unconventional and Amazing Guitar Chords,
Professional Techniques, Capo Tricks,
Alternate Tunings, Head Math, Rhythm & More

MICAH BROOKS

MICAH BROOKS

WORSHIPHEART

PUBLISHING | EST. 1985

© 2016 | WorshipHeart Publishing
All Rights Reserved.
ISBN: 0997194057
ISBN-978-0-9971940-5-0

Copyright Information

Published by WorshipHeart Publishing

© 2016 Micah Brooks Kennedy | WorshipHeart Publishing

All rights herein, both implied and expressed, are reserved. No part of this book may be reproduced or transmitted in any form without prior written consent from WorshipHeart Publishing. This includes any means electronic or mechanical, such as photocopying. Violators will be prosecuted.

For written permission contact WorshipHeart Publishing at: www.worshippublishing.com or email info@worshippublishing.com

Drawings by Micah Brooks Kennedy and Amy Roberts

Proof Editing by Mary Davis

ISBN #: 978-0-9971940-5-0

MICAH BROOKS

Recommendations

Praise for Micah Brooks & *Guitar Secrets Revealed*

"Micah Brooks is an amazing teacher of not only elements, building blocks and tools but application. This book will show you what you need to know and how to do it well with results. Micah makes the hard work less hard."

-**Jared Anderson** Christian Artist and Songwriter of *Great I Am*, *Amazed* and *Rescue*

"I know of no other guitar book like this one! In *Guitar Secrets Revealed*, you'll benefit from insider tips and tricks learned throughout Micah's years of experience. This is a book every guitarist should have on their shelf."

-**Dave Tanner** Founder of Retail Bookstore Christian Publishers Outlet www.christianpublishersoutlet.com

"This is a cool book! There are tips in this one that everyone can appreciate. From interesting chords to some music pro knowledge that is important, I recommend *Guitar Secrets Revealed* to every guitarist. Essential."

-**Dylan Rosson** Lead Guitarist for American Idol's Scotty McCreery

"Micah has become a good friend of us here at worshipministry.com and he's written another great book! *Guitar Secrets Revealed* offers the guitarist the inside scoop that would take ten years of working out for yourself to learn. You learn really cool chords, neat uses of the capo and crucial music theory that every player should know. I recommend this book to anyone looking to become a better guitar player!"

-**Gary Miller** Executive Director for www.worshipministry.com

"Do you want to make the leap from an amateur guitar player to an accomplished one? This will mean acquiring a whole new set of skills that will take years to master but Micah Brook's new book, *Guitar Secrets Revealed* will shorten the journey. This book will unveil the secrets of guitar playing that professional players employ and might I add, closely guard. Now you can benefit from Micah's "tricks", as he calls them, and consequently very soon your guitar playing will take on a whole new level of enjoyment. To put it bluntly, you cannot be without this book!"

-**Rev. Malcolm Hedding** Associate Minister World Outreach Church
Executive Director Emeritus
The International Christian Embassy Jerusalem

"Help!" Have you ever been there with your guitar in hand? This is the tool book that you need to expand your chord knowledge, find out about alternate tunings, capo options and so much more. I LOVE that it teaches you the number system. It will simplify your ability to play a song in any key. If you're serious about being a musician this book is a must read.

-**Yancy** Artist, Songwriter and Worship Leader for Families
www.yancyministries.com

"As a worship pastor and piano player, I have a hard time explaining to my guitarists how to play the "complicated" chords. This book really dives into those kinds of chords: like minor 7 and "add9". Also, the capo charts are a great reference for any guitarist, whether advanced or beginner. This book is an all-around great tool!"

-**Kevin Kruse** Worship Pastor Laurelwood Baptist Church; Vancouver, WA

"*Guitar Secrets Revealed* is the perfect book for the guitarist who wants to keep up with the pros. In this book, you'll learn the techniques and theory that professionals use daily. The material covered in this book is great for the guitarist at any level and will expand your arsenal of knowledge. If you want to save years of trial and error, this book can help."

-**Harrison Brock** Current Micah Brooks Guitar Student (Age 16)

Dedication

It is a great honor to dedicate this book to my family. My wife, Rochelle, allows me to pursue my passions while supporting me along the way. Our three children, Liam, Aisley and Jovie are wonderful and will hopefully learn this material themselves someday. I love you all and pray for you daily.

In This Series and Additional Resources

Find out about the other books in this series and sign up for the Micah Brooks "Stay Connected" mailing list.

This is book two in the Micah Brooks Guitar Authority Series books. *Worship Guitar In Six Weeks* is a six week course designed to bring a guitar player from knowing little about guitar onto the stage in six weeks. Please pass it along to your friends! Also, the next book in this series is called *Guitar Secrets Revealed*. Learn what the guitar professionals know without needing to spend years to acquire that information. Find out about the Micah Brooks Guitar Authority Series books and more at:

www.micahbrooks.com

Email Micah

Email Micah Brooks at micah@micahbrooks.com. I want to know who you are. I have a heart to meet people. It is my privilege to respond to my emails personally. Please feel free to connect with me. I will glad to answer questions or set up a Skype call as you need.

Join the Micah Brooks "Stay Connected" mailing list to stay up to date

Subscribe to the Micah Brooks Ministry "Stay Connected" mailing list and stay current with my latest book releases. My email list is always free and intended to deliver high value content to your inbox. I do not sell your email address to anyone else. I simply want to be able to stay connected with you. Click here to join my mailing list.

www.micahbrooks.com/join

Reviews on Amazon

Reviews are the lifeblood of authors. If you are willing to leave feedback, I would be humbled and grateful. Please do so at www.amazon.com

Skype Lessons

I would be glad to consider giving you online guitar lessons. If you would like to apply for lessons with Micah Brooks via Skype visit my website to find out more. I cannot accept every student, but I would be happy to hear your story and see what you would like to accomplish.

www.micahbrooks.com

Join The Christian Guitar Community Facebook Group

All readers of this book are welcome to join The Christian Guitar Community Facebook group. Meet guitar players from around the world. You may post your insights about learning guitar. You are welcome to ask questions and comment on other posts. The group is designed to be a community. We ask everyone in the group to interact, which makes the content fun and engaging.

www.facebook.com/groups/thechristianguitarcommunity

More About Micah Brooks Ministry

For more about Micah Brooks and my ministry, including books, CDs, mp3s, clothing and art designs, online store, blogs, devotions, speaking and performing dates please go to:

www.micahbrooks.com

Follow Micah Brooks

Everyone is welcome to follow Micah Brooks on these social media platforms:

Facebook: @micahbrookspage
www.facebook.com/micahbrookspage

Twitter: @mchbrks
www.twitter.com/mchbrks

LinkedIn: Micah Brooks
www.linkedin.com/in/micahbrooks

Instagram: @mchbrks
www.instagram.com/mchbrks

If you have trouble connecting to any of these social media accounts, please visit www.micahbrooks.com.

Micah is Editor In Chief at www.worshippublishing.com, www.uprightpassiveincome.com and www.songwritingcreative.com

Worship Publishing is a resource website that includes books, daily devotions, music, podcasts, product reviews and many more recommendations. Use our wealth of staff writers and high quality guest post content to better your walk with the Lord. Visit: www.worshippublishing.com

Upright Passive Income is a company devoted to helping entrepreneurs achieve their vision and dreams. Everyone should have a side business of some kind and earning passive income is an awesome way to do so. Great examples include self-publishing a book, affiliate marketing and video marketing. Visit: www.uprightpassiveincome.com to learn about all of our high quality services.

Songwriting Creative is a website devoted to songwriting in all forms. From beginner writers to the most advanced, we each still have room to grow and expand our skills and craft. www.songwritingcreative.com is intended to be a songwriting community and we do our best to facilitate. Check it out.

Table Of Contents

Introduction — 15
Chapter ONE: Barre Chords Using The Thumb — 21
Chapter TWO: "E5" and Related Chords — 29
Chapter THREE: "Eadd9" and Related Chords — 35
Chapter FOUR: "B" Using The Thumb and Related Chords — 41
G, D and C Section Notes — 47
Chapter FIVE: "G5" and Related Chords — 49
Chapter SIX: "D" and Related Chords — 55
Chapter SEVEN: "C" and Related Chords — 61
Chapter EIGHT: Strange But Cool Chords — 67
Practical Application Sections — 73
Chapter NINE: Head Math (How To Use Numbers and The Capo To Play In Other Keys) — 75
Chapter TEN: The Awesome Use Of The Capo — 85
Chapter ELEVEN: Transitioning Chords Quickly — 97
Chapter TWELVE: The Amazing Guitar Pick — 101
Chapter THIRTEEN: Alternate Guitar Tunings — 105
Chapter FOURTEEN: How To Notate Guitar Music — 111
Chapter FIFTEEN: How To Play Rhythm Guitar In A Band — 113
Final Greetings — 117
In This Series and Additional Resources — 119
Appendix — 123
About The Author — 129

Introduction

Welcome to *Guitar Secrets Revealed: Unconventional and Amazing Guitar Chords, Professional Techniques, Capo Tricks, Alternate Tunings, Head Math, Rhythm & More*

Before we begin, I sincerely thank you for purchasing this book. I want to get to know you and am available via email at micah@micahbrooks.com. If you have any questions, want to get to know me, or want more clarification as you work through this book, please do not hesitate to connect with me. I want to be as available to you as I know how. It is in my heart to do so.

This book is the third in my guitar books series. Truly this is the culmination of everything I have accumulated in my guitar learning over the last nearly twenty years of playing. In preparing for this book I kept saying that this is for intermediate to professional level players. Intermediate guitarists will learn a lot. Professionals will learn something too because I am sure there are a few unconventional methods of playing chords in here that you may not even know yet. Conversely, I bet you could write a book that would have the same effect on me and I would like to buy your book. Iron sharpens iron, baby!

The goal of this book is to share some unconventional guitar chords that you would not normally learn from a traditional guitar lesson. These are the types of chords you only develop over many years of playing the instrument. Some of them are unconventional. All of them are awesome! I hope that this book is a shortcut for you learning some really fun guitar chords. You will not need to spend twenty years developing these. You can move on to even more.

I have written this book as if you and I were sitting together casually. I use the first person voice and am intentional to speak with you as the real person you are. This is a practical manual and not a lesson in English or grammar. My goal is for you to learn the material.

Let's Pray!

I begin every guitar lesson and every meeting that I am in charge of with prayer. If you do not mind, I would like to pray for you before we begin this book. As a worship leader as my main profession, it is a part of my genetic makeup. I am not asking you to convert, just that if there is a God and he can help us learn, that he will do so now. No worries.

"Lord Jesus, I thank You for my new reader. May he or she develop several new guitar chords and techniques while reading this book. Watch over them and guard them. May their time be fruitful. Thank You. In Jesus' name, amen."

How to use this book

This book assumes you know the basics, like the chords "G", "C" and "D". I am careful to still explain every chord that you learn in this book, but if you are completely new to the guitar, I recommend my first book *Worship Guitar In Six Weeks* and then my other book *42 Guitar Chords Everyone Should Know* first. This book is full of fun alternative ways to play some of the basic chords that are assumed you already know and so much more!

I have arranged this manual so that you can jump around, however, some of the chords are related to the ones that have either come before or after them. Also, some of the chords are movable, which means that I have shown you how to play the chord at one position on the neck, but it can be moved up or down the neck to create many more chords. You will need to experiment.

Unconventional

Please note that many of the chords use the thumb which you may or may not have ever used before on the left fretting hand. You may even say that the recommendations within this book are unconventional. You would be right! In a typical guitar lesson, I would not teach a beginning student these chords that I am about to show you. However, these are a professional's guide into accessing chords faster than some of the more traditional methods.

Please note that all of these chords have been written assuming a right-handed guitar player. If you are a southpaw, you're still awesome! Assume your right hand rather than how I have written this book for left hand and you should be able to fret these chords.

Also within this book are some ways to play in alternate tunings that may be new to you. An alternate tuning is literally an alternate way to tune your guitar rather than the standard EADGBe method. Most of the time an alternate tuning allows you to play in what is known as an open way. In fact, you may be able to strum the guitar without your fretting hand on the guitar at all and hear a rich, full chord. The Goo Goo Dolls are a notorious example of using open tunings in nearly all of their songs.

There is a section related to using your capo in ways you may not know about. Normally a capo is a tool that you place in between frets to raise the nut, thus allowing you to play more standard chords but raising the key. In my unusual capo section, you will find ways to use the capo to make the guitar sound more open. I also recommend purchasing a cut capo made by Kyser. There will be more on that in the capo section.

I have included a guitar pick section to give you an idea of ways to use a guitar pick that you may or may not have ever thought of. This includes changing sizes of picks, the type of material used and ways to hold a pick.

Depending on what you want to accomplish with your guitar, the section on head math and numbers may be the most important section for you. This section teaches you how to memorize songs quickly. This is the most plain and simple, down-to-earth music theory lesson you are every going to experience.

Do not forget to check out the bonus sections that include how to buy a guitar at a guitar store and how to use a locking method to change your guitar strings that will keep your strings from going out of tune. You may or may not be doing all that you need to in order to clean and maintain your guitar. Do not forget the appendix.

Chord Diagram

Every chord has a unique chord diagram. There are several parts in each one. In this section they are explained. Refer back to this diagram as you begin learning. We have also shot photos of our team playing the various chords in this book. Between the two references, you should be able to master any chord we propose.

Chord Diagram Explained

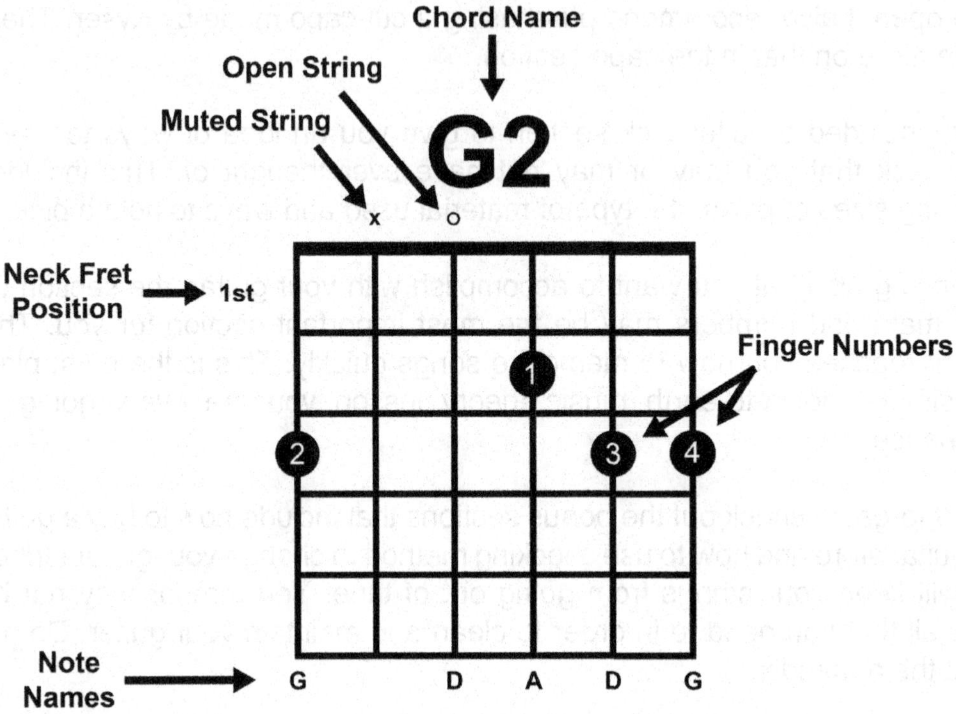
Chord Name
Open String
Muted String
G2
x
o
Neck Fret Position
1st
Finger Numbers
1
2
3
4
Note Names
G
D
A
D
G

Chord Name

This section is to describe the name of the chord. This may include a chord suffix, like "C6" where the "6" is the modifier.

Open String

An open string is a guitar string that is played with no finger touching it. The note name is the string's name. For example, if you play an open fourth string (like in this "G2" chord example), the open note being played on the [D] string is a "D".

Muted String

A muted string is one that is either being muted by a neighboring finger or intentionally not being played with the right, strumming hand. In this example of the "G2" chord, the fifth string [A] is not being played.

Neck Fret Position

The neck fret position number is important to always notice when reviewing a chord diagram. That number signifies the starting position of your fingers on the neck. It can go as high as the last fret on your guitar. If you see a "1st" denotation, then the chord is played in open position at the beginning of the neck. "1st" is the *home base* position on the guitar. Everything else is related to that home base position. Were you to see "3rd", like in a "C#" chord, then your root note begins on the fourth fret. Do your best to observe the neck fret position indication for each chord.

Finger Numbers

While you could use nicknames for each finger on your left hand (like index finger, pinky, etc.) most guitar teachers will use numbers for each finger. Using numbers allows for quick reference as you get into chord diagrams and transitioning.

Here is how I detail each finger of the left hand. The index finger (index finger) is (1). Your middle finger is (2), ring finger is (3) and pinky finger (4). I label the thumb (T). While you will not get into any thumb playing in this book, you may as you improve in your skills moving on to further chording. Note: left-handed guitarists will use the opposite hand, making each of the labels above true for the *right hand* rather than the left.

Note Names

Below each chord diagram are the note names being played per string. Please notice that these are not the root names of the strings when being played open. Rather, these are the notes being played after fretting the chord. Some of the notes will be the open notes, but only when there is no finger needed for that particular string in the chord. When a string is being omitted or muted, no note name will be present.

It's time to dive in! Let's go!

Chapter ONE: Barre Chords Using The Thumb

Why in the world would you use your thumb?

Using the thumb of the left fretting hand may be the least traditional way to play guitar chords. However, perhaps it is better said that using the thumb is the most underutilized finger you have to choose from. As long as your hand is large enough to grip around the neck of your guitar then you are welcome to use the thumb as the fifth fretting finger (the 3 F's, ha!).

"F" chords using the thumb

Traditionally, you would play an "F" chord by barring across the entire first fret with your index finger (1). The advantage of using the thumb (T) instead is to limit the amount of barring that the index finger (1) is required to do and also to move quickly to and from an "Fsus" chord. The images below demonstrate the difference between a traditional "F" chord and the thumbed "F" chord. Also see the "Fsus" chord played using both types of barres.

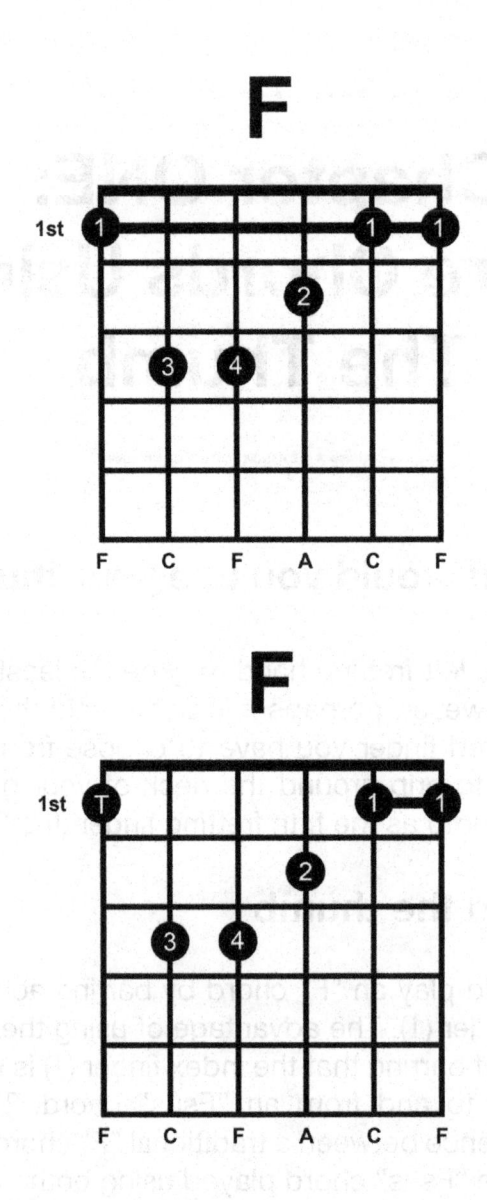

How to fret an "F" chord using the thumb

Begin by placing your index finger (1) as a barre across the first frets of both the second [B] and the first [e] strings. It is important to keep a firm hold of those two notes. They may have a tendency to become loose causing deadened upper strings. Next, add your ring finger (3) to the third fret of the fifth string [A]. Following that, add your pinky finger (4) to the third fret of the fourth string [D]. Now add your middle finger (2) to the second fret of the third string [G]. Last, and this is where the chord becomes unconventional, place your thumb [T] on the first fret of the sixth string [E]. You now need to make sure your grip is strong across all frets and strings. Strum all six strings to play an "F". As with any chord you learn in this book, (or in life) the best way to master a chord is through practice. Fret the "F" chord then take your entire left hand off the guitar and build it again. You will know you have mastered it when, and only when, you can place your fingers into position in one motion. When all fingers fall into place simultaneously. Until you reach that point you still need to practice the chord.

What can I do with this?

The benefit of playing an "F" chord in this unconventional way is how easy it is to strum between "F" and "Fsus". After you have fretted an "F" using the thumb you can move your middle finger (2) to the place where your ring finger (3) was (the third fret of the fifth string [A]). Move that ring finger (3) from the fifth string [A] to the fourth string [D] fret three. Move your pinky finger (4) from that fifth string [A] fret to the third fret of the third string [G]. This makes transitioning between "F" and "Fsus" a bit simpler than when you fret these "F's" with a full barre across fret one using the index finger (1).

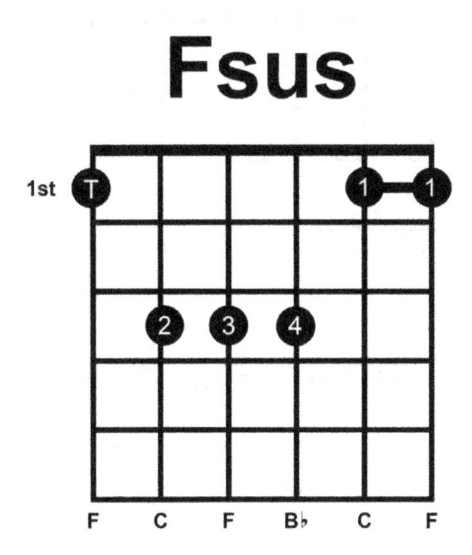

Fsus

What else can I do with this?

The other amazing benefit of learning this unconventional method for the "F" and "Fsus" is that this barre chord is moveable. If you move your entire left hand up one fret then you will be playing an "F#" ("G♭") and "F#sus" ("G♭sus"). Move the hand up two frets and you will have a "G" and "Gsus". Move up to the fifth fret and you have an "A" and "Asus" and so on. By learning this one technique you will have equipped yourself with over thirty chords. Fantastic!

"B♭" chords using the thumb

Continuing on with our incredible use of the thumb, you can also play a "B♭" chord using the thumb, rather than the traditional barre version. The two benefits of using this method is either this becomes how you play a "B♭" going forward or it is how quickly you can transition to a "B♭2". You may even want to play a "B♭2" by itself, having transitioned from your thumbed "F".

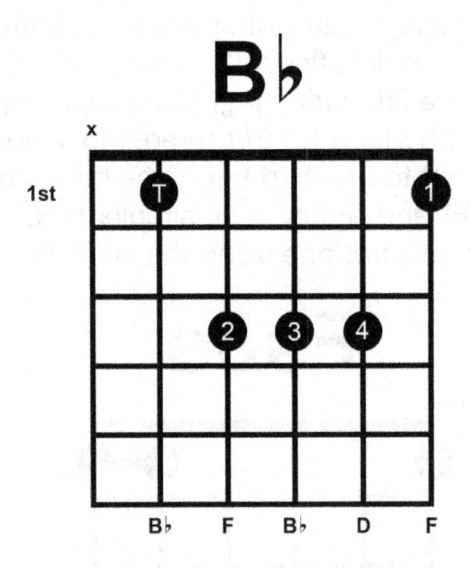

How to fret a "B♭" chord using the thumb

First, as with the the "F" played with the thumb, begin by placing your index finger (1) onto the first fret of the first string [e]. Next, in series, add your middle finger (2), ring finger (3) and pinky finger (4) to the third frets of the fourth [D], third [G] and second [B] strings. Those will need to form a tight package or you may encounter fret buzz. Last, add your thumb (T) to the first fret of the fifth string [A]. Notice that you will need to mute the sixth string [E] with your thumb. As you become a natural at playing this chord you will mostly likely mute that note as second nature. Initially you may need to be careful not to produce sound on that string. Muting that sixth string [E], strum across all six strings. You will only be hearing sound out of five though. This is a "B♭" chord played by using the thumb.

B♭2

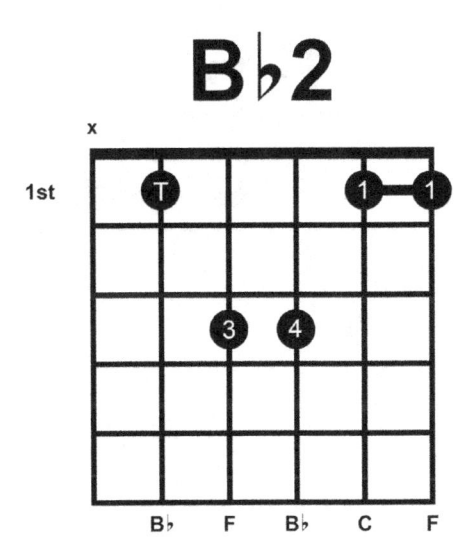

To build a "B♭2", simply take off your pinky finger (4) and barre the last two strings [B] and [e] with your index finger (1). This chord transitions to and from the thumbed "F" chord easily and sounds wonderful.

As with the thumbed "F" chords, the "B♭" chords you have just learned are moveable. Begin on the first fret and you have the "B♭". Move to the third fret and you have built a "C" chord. Onto the fifth fret and you have a "D" chord and so on. By learning this fingering position you have learned another thirty or so chords. So far in about three pages we have learned over sixty chords. Wow! Find someone and ask them to give you a round of applause.

"Fm" and "B♭m" chords using the thumb

Since we have learned both the "F" and the "B♭" in their various forms, we can very easily add both "Fm" and "B♭m".

Fm

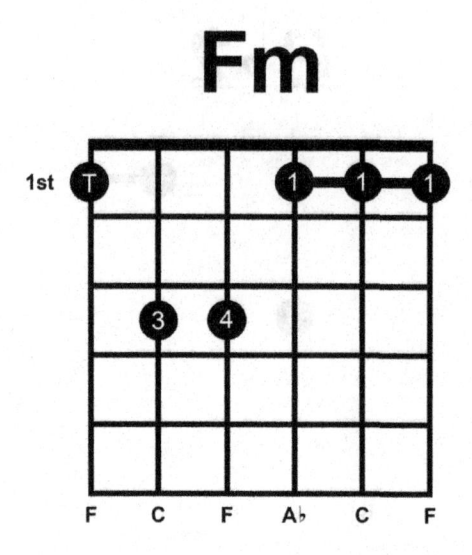

```
         F  C  F  Ab C  F
1st  T        1--1--1
              
           3  4
```

To build an "Fm" using the thumb, first begin by fretting the thumbed "F" chord. You then remove your middle finger (2) from the third string [G]. Last you need to extend your barre with your index finger (1) that is currently across the second [B] and first [e] strings to the third string [G] on the first fret. Strum all six strings and you have an "Fm" chord.

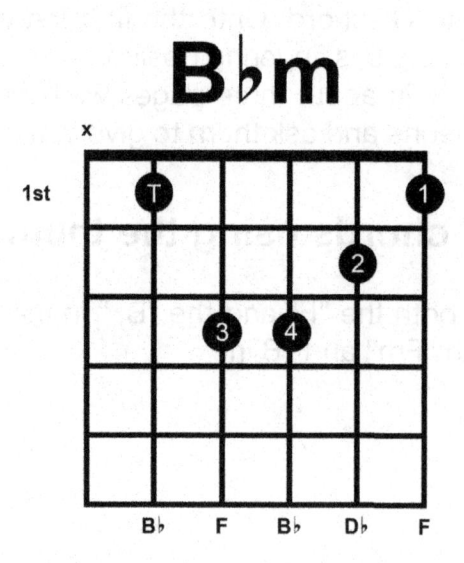

B♭m

```
      x
         Bb F  Bb Db F
1st      T           1
                  2
              3  4
```

To construct the thumbed "B♭m" chord mentioned above, first fret your "B♭2" chord. Simply add your middle finger (2) to the second fret of the second string [B] and you have built an easy "B♭m". Strum just like you did the other "B♭" chords you have learned. Strum across all six strings, muting the lowest sixth string [E].

Both the "Fm" and "B♭m" are moveable in the same ways as "F" and "B♭". Move to the third frets of either and you have built a "Gm" and "Cm". Move to the fifth frets and you have made an "Am" and "Dm". That means you have added another sixty chords to your chord library. We are already at over one hundred and twenty chords and we have not broken a sweat. The guitar is such a versatile instrument.

Chapter TWO: "E5" and Related Chords

Playing in an open key of E style

This next section may be familiar to more seasoned guitarists, except for the last chord in the series. Playing in the key of E is like the pianist's key of C. It is a very natural guitar key. This is an open way to play in the key of E that sounds amazing. You will learn the five important chords that make up just about every pop song: the 1, 2m, 4, 5 and 6m. If that concept is foreign to you, check out the section is this book called "Head Math".

Each of these next five chords have two open strings that remain throughout. This is what makes them so smooth sounding and easy to use. Also, these are all open chords. That means that at least two of the strings are left open at all times, but there could be more, allowing the guitar to sustain longer than when using barre chords. Use these chords to play just about any pop or worship song.

"E5"

We begin with the "E5" chord. It is the basis or foundation for all of the others in this five chord series. By the end of learning these five you will understand why this is so.

E5

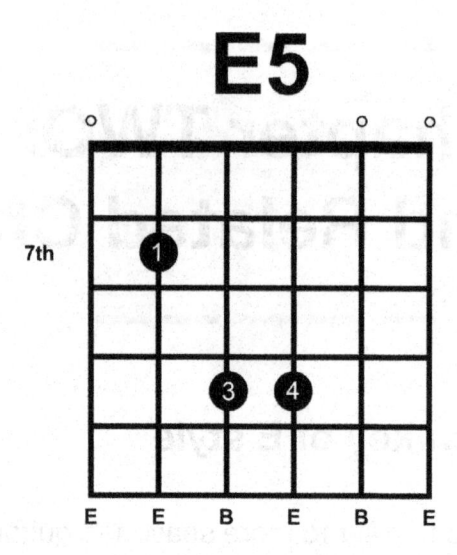

```
        o           o   o
    ┌───┬───┬───┬───┬───┐
7th │ 1 │   │   │   │   │
    ├───┼───┼───┼───┼───┤
    │   │   │   │   │   │
    ├───┼───┼───┼───┼───┤
    │   │ 3 │ 4 │   │   │
    ├───┼───┼───┼───┼───┤
    │   │   │   │   │   │
    └───┴───┴───┴───┴───┘
     E   E   B   E   B   E
```

To fret an "E5" chord, begin by placing your index finger (1) on to the seventh fret of the fifth string [A]. Next add your ring finger (3) and your pinky finger (4) to the ninth frets of the fourth and third strings, respectively. Your middle finger is not used in this chord, but will be so as we progress. Strum all six strings, beginning at the bottom, sixth string [E]. This chord should sound very clean and strong. Again, it is the basis for all of the others that follow.

"C#m7"

C#m7

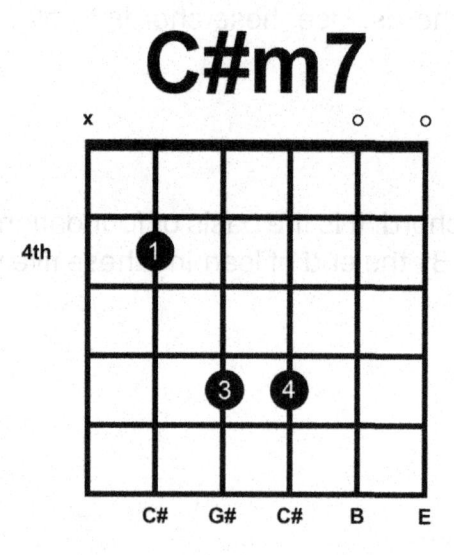

```
      x           o   o
    ┌───┬───┬───┬───┬───┐
4th │ 1 │   │   │   │   │
    ├───┼───┼───┼───┼───┤
    │   │   │   │   │   │
    ├───┼───┼───┼───┼───┤
    │   │ 3 │ 4 │   │   │
    ├───┼───┼───┼───┼───┤
    │   │   │   │   │   │
    └───┴───┴───┴───┴───┘
     C#  G#  C#  B   E
```

Once we have successfully built an "E5" chord we can move everything down three frets to create a "C#m7". Your index finger (1) will now be on the fourth fret of the fifth string [A] and your ring (3) and pinky (4) fingers on the sixth frets of the fourth [D] and third [G] strings. This time you need to omit the low sixth string [E] and strum only the last five strings, beginning with the fifth string [A]. In doing so you are now playing a full "C#m7" chord. Practice playing an "E5" and then sliding downward three frets to a "C#m7".

"Bsus"

Bsus

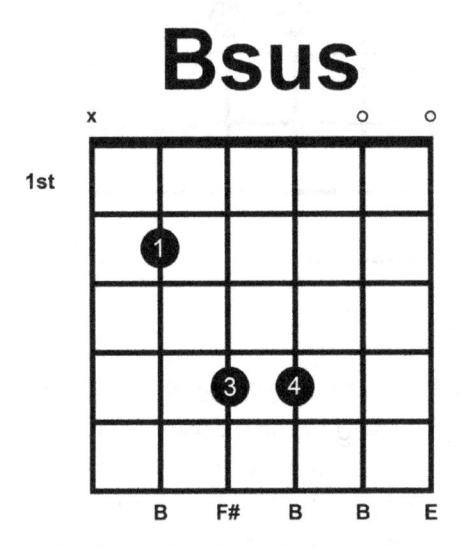

```
x           o   o
    ┌─┬─┬─┬─┬─┐
1st │ │ │ │ │ │
    ├─┼─┼─┼─┼─┤
    │①│ │ │ │ │
    ├─┼─┼─┼─┼─┤
    │ │ │ │ │ │
    ├─┼─┼─┼─┼─┤
    │ │ │③│④│ │
    ├─┼─┼─┼─┼─┤
    │ │ │ │ │ │
    └─┴─┴─┴─┴─┘
    B  F#  B  B  E
```

As we move further down the neck we can create a "Bsus" chord by transitioning downward by two more frets. Now your index finger (1) will be on the second fret of the fifth string [A] and your ring (3) and pinky (4) fingers on the fourth frets of the fourth [D] and third [G] strings respectively. As with the "C#m7", you need only strum the last five strings. Now you should be able to practice playing an "E5" to a "C#m7" and then on to the "Bsus".

"A2"

A2

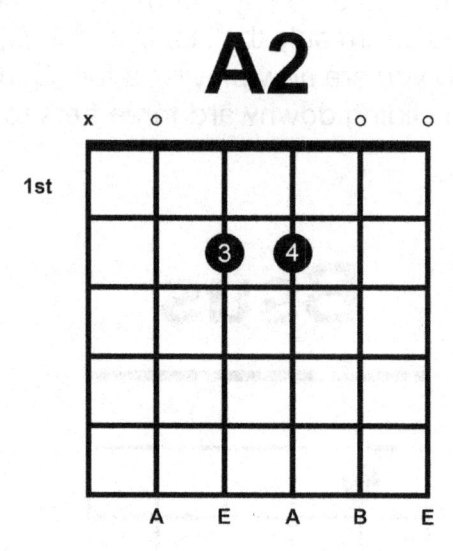

```
  x  o     o  o
┌──┬──┬──┬──┬──┐
│  │  │  │  │  │  1st
├──┼──┼──┼──┼──┤
│  │  │ ③│ ④│  │
├──┼──┼──┼──┼──┤
│  │  │  │  │  │
├──┼──┼──┼──┼──┤
│  │  │  │  │  │
├──┼──┼──┼──┼──┤
│  │  │  │  │  │
└──┴──┴──┴──┴──┘
  A  E  A  B  E
```

Now onto one last move down the neck so that your index finger (1) comes off the neck entirely and your ring (3) and pinky (4) fingers land on the second frets of the fourth [D] and third [G] strings. This is an "A2" chord. You may have learned this chord before, but using your index (1) and middle (2) fingers. This time we are using the ring (3) and pinky (4) fingers to play the same chord. This is because it makes it easy to transition to and from our "Bsus" chord or any of the others where the ring (3) and pinky (4) fingers are side by side. Strum only the last five strings, beginning with the fifth string [A].

"F#m7"

F#m7

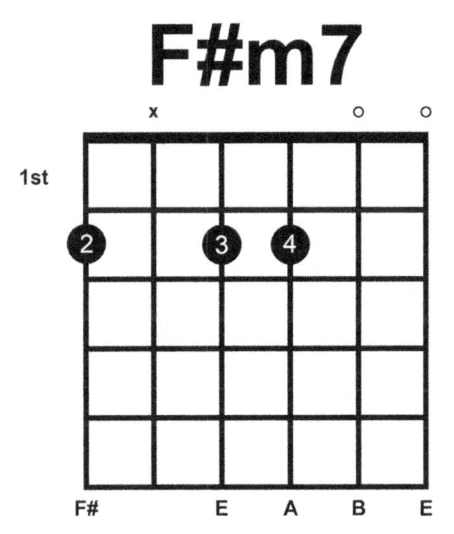

```
x       o o
1st
  |  ②  |  ③ ④  |
  |     |        |
  |     |        |
  |     |        |
 F#    E  A  B  E
```

The last chord in this series is an "F#m7". First build the "A2" chord we learned in the previous section. Next, place your middle finger (2) on the second fret of the sixth string [E]. This forms an "F#m7" by strumming across all six strings. Notice that you should be muting the fifth string [A] with your middle finger (2). Were you not to mute it the "F#m7" will still sound, it just will not be as clear as when you mute that fifth string [A].

Practice all five chords

You now have learned "E5", "C#m7", "Bsus", "A2" and "F#m7" chords. Practice transitioning in and out of all of them from one to the others. You never know which combination you may be required to use. You want to be an expert at each. Notice how the second [B] and first [e] strings remain open in all five chords. This helps to keep the series sounding smooth.

You may add a capo to the first fret, moving each of these chords up one fret to play an "F5", "Dm7", "Csus", "B♭2" and "Gm7". Move the capo up three frets from the open position, moving your fingers up three frets as well and you will have a "G5", "Em7", "Dsus", "C2" and "Am7". In essence, you have learned another twenty-five or more chords, depending on the length of your guitar neck, by using this series of chords and your capo. Rock on!

Chapter THREE: "Eadd9" and Related Chords

Playing in a second open key of E style beginning with an "Eadd9" chord that many have never played

In the previous chapter we learned how to play in an open key of E style using the "E5" chord. In this chapter will learn to play in a similar style, but built from a very special "Eadd9" chord. Very few guitarists know this chord. However, the "Eadd9" sounds amazing and the chords that follow play wonderfully, too.

"Eadd9"

Eadd9

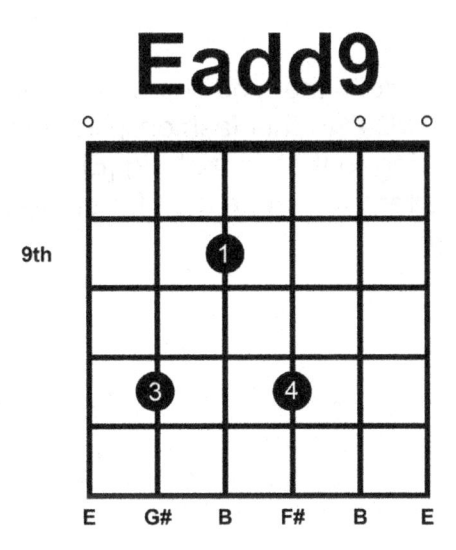

9th

E G# B F# B E

To build an "Eadd9", begin by placing your ring finger (3) on the eleventh fret of the fifth string [A]. Next, add your index finger (1) to the ninth fret of the fourth string [D]. Last, add your pinky finger (4) to the eleventh fret of the third string [G] and strum all six strings. This chord sounds unique and beautiful.

There is a richness because of the "add9" part of the chord. The ninth note of the scale is being added to a standard "E5" chord.

As in the previous chapter, we can now take this new "Eadd9" chord and build the series of 1, 4, 5 and 6m, but this time a few modifications are necessary.

"B/D#"

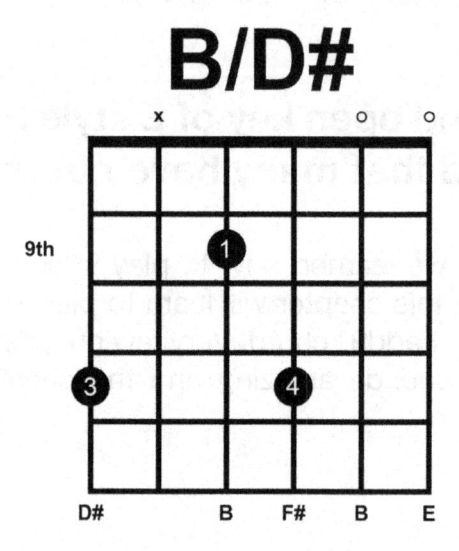

```
            B/D#
         x       o    o

9th      ┌──┬──┬──┬──┬──┐
         │  │  │  │  │  │
         ├──┼──●──┼──┼──┤
         │  │  │  │  │  │
         ├──┼──┼──┼──┼──┤
         │  │  │  │  │  │
         ●──┼──┼──●──┼──┤
         │ 3│  │ 4│  │  │
         ├──┼──┼──┼──┼──┤
         D#    B  F#  B  E
```

The next chord after the "Eadd9" that you should learn is the quick transition to the "B/D#". To play a "B/D#" in this fashion you only need to move your ring finger (3) down one string to the sixth string [E]. Remain on the eleventh fret. In doing so, you will effectively mute the fifth string [A]. Strum across all six strings to form a "B/D#".

"C#m7" chord with the thumb

C#m7

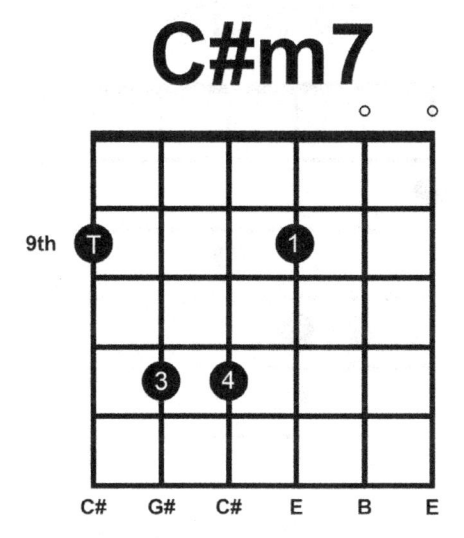

(chord diagram: 9th fret, T on 6th string, 1 on 3rd string at 9th fret, 3 and 4 on 5th and 4th strings at 11th fret; 2nd and 1st strings open)

C# G# C# E B E

To transition to the next chord, we need to build a "C#m7" by using the thumb [T]. Like other thumbed chords, this one is unconventional, but awesome. Begin by placing your ring (3) and pinky (4) fingers onto the eleventh frets of the fifth [A] and fourth [D] strings respectively. Next, place your index finger (1) on the ninth fret of the third string [G]. Last, add your thumb (T) to the ninth fret of the sixth string [E]. Strum across all six strings. Make sure that the last two strings, the second [B] and first [e] are left open. That is the brilliance of the unconventional "C#m7".

"Bsus" chord with the thumb

The next two chords that we will learn fret similarly and sound great. First, we must build a special "Bsus" chord. The power in both of these chords is just like the three chords that have gone before in that the upper two strings have been left open.

Bsus

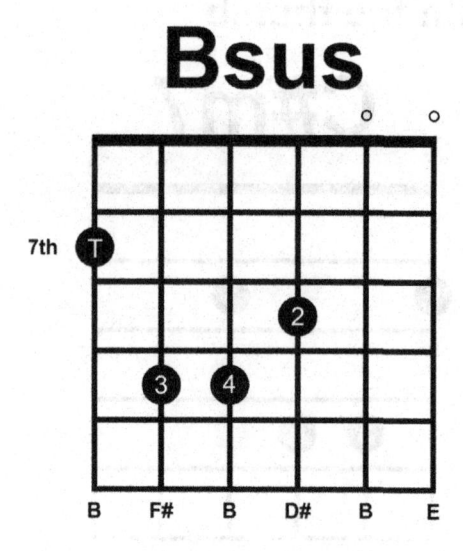

To build a "Bsus" chord, begin by placing your thumb (T) on to the seventh fret of the sixth string [E]. Next, add your ring (3) and pinky (4) fingers to the ninth fret of the fifth [A] and fourth [D] strings, respectively. Last, add your middle finger (2) to the eighth fret of the third string [G]. Strum across all six strings as you have in all of the other chords in this series. This is "Bsus".

"A2" chord with the thumb

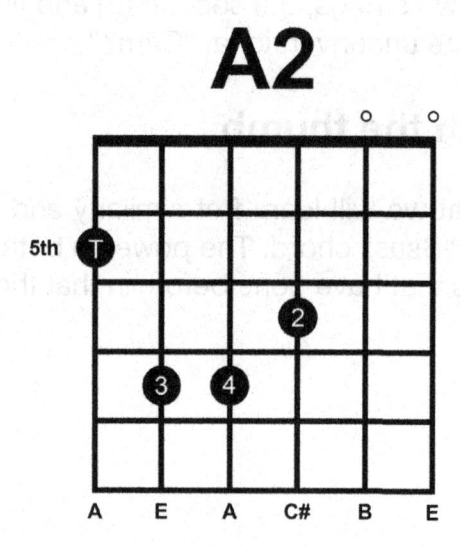

A2

For our final chord in this series move all four fingers down two frets on the same strings when coming from the "Bsus" to produce a special "A2" chord. Were you building the chord from scratch and not transitioning downward it would build like this: Place your thumb (T) on to the fifth fret of the sixth string [E]. Next, add your ring (3) and pinky (4) fingers to the seventh fret of the fifth [A] and fourth [D] strings, respectively. Last, add your middle finger (2) to the sixth fret of the third string [G]. Strum across all six strings to create this "A2" chord.

Use all five chords to play hundreds of songs

All five of the chords in the "Eadd9" series can be used to play hundreds of songs. Effectively you have built a 1, 5/7, 6m, 5 and 4 chord. Practice playing them all. Add a capo on the first fret to play in the key of F by moving your fingers up one fret each. Add the capo to fret two and play in "F#" moving the fingers up two frets from the initial "Eadd9" position and so on.

Chapter FOUR: "B" Using The Thumb and Related Chords

Playing in the key of B on guitar can seem like a barre chord nightmare. Not anymore...

Just about every guitar player I know would rather not play in the key of B because there are so few open chords you can play. To play full, six string chords in the key of B it is normally played as six and five string barre chords. In this chapter I will introduce a new method of playing in the key of B that uses the thumb and are all open chords. I use this method almost every time I play and now I love playing in the key of B.

"B5" chord with the thumb

This "B5" chord is the foundational chord for all the following. Make sure you learn this chord the best you can before moving forward.

B5

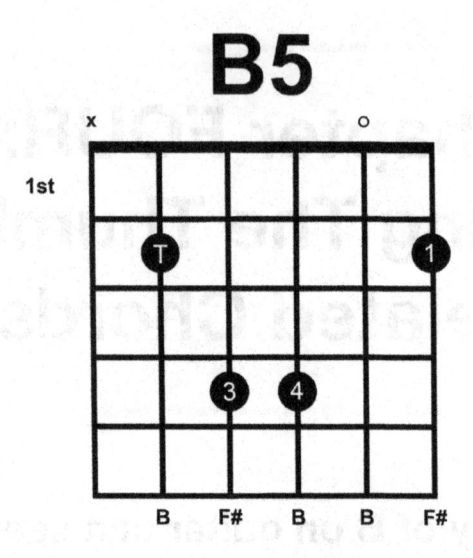

Begin by placing your thumb (T) on to the second fret of the fifth string [A]. Next, place your ring (3) and pinky (4) fingers on the fourth frets of the fourth [D] and third [G] strings, respectively. Last, add your index finger (1) to the second fret of the first string [e]. You will strum only the last five strings beginning with the fifth string [A], omitting the sixth string [E]. Please note that the second string [B] needs to remain open. This is how you play an open sounding "B5" chord.

"F#sus" chord with the thumb

F#sus

Deriving from the new "B5" chord you just learned, we move on to the "F#sus" open chord. Begin by forming the "B5" chord. Next, remove your pinky finger (4) from the third string [G], replacing it with your middle finger (2) on the third fret of that same string. Last, move your thumb (T) from the second fret of the fifth string [A] to the second fret of the sixth string [E]. You will effectively mute the fifth string [A] now. Strum across all six strings and you will create an open "F#sus" chord.

"G#m7"

G#m7

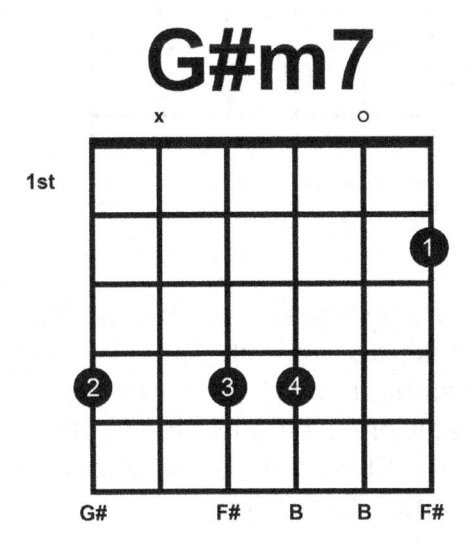

```
           x         o
      ┌──┬──┬──┬──┐
 1st  │  │  │  │  │
      ├──┼──┼──┼──┤
      │  │  │  │ ①│
      ├──┼──┼──┼──┤
      │  │  │  │  │
      ├──┼──┼──┼──┤
      │② │  │③ │④ │
      ├──┼──┼──┼──┤
      │  │  │  │  │
      └──┴──┴──┴──┘
      G#    F# B  B  F#
```

To build the "G#m7" open chord, please begin with your open "B5" chord from the beginning of this chapter. Next, simply move your middle finger (2) that was not being used in the "B5" chord to the fourth fret of the sixth string [E]. Your thumb is no longer needed for this chord. You will mute the fifth string [A]. This may occur naturally with your middle finger (2). Strum across all six strings to form an open "G#m7" chord.

"E2"

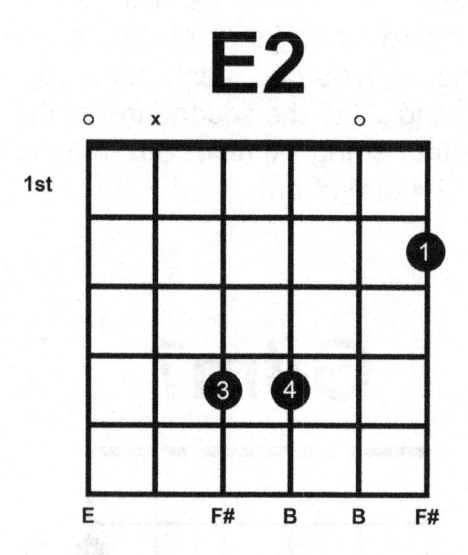

E2

(chord diagram: 1st fret; notes from low to high: E (open), x, F#, B, B, F#; fingers 3 on 4th string, 4 on 3rd string, 1 on 1st string)

The next chord also begins by building your initial "B5" chord. To make an "E2" chord you simply take your thumb off of the second fret of the fifth string [A] and mute that string. I usually mute that string with a gentle touch from my ring finger (3) that is pressing down the fourth fret of the fourth string [D]. Now your lowest string [E] is open. Strum across all six strings, muting the fifth string [A], for an open "E2" chord.

"C#m7"

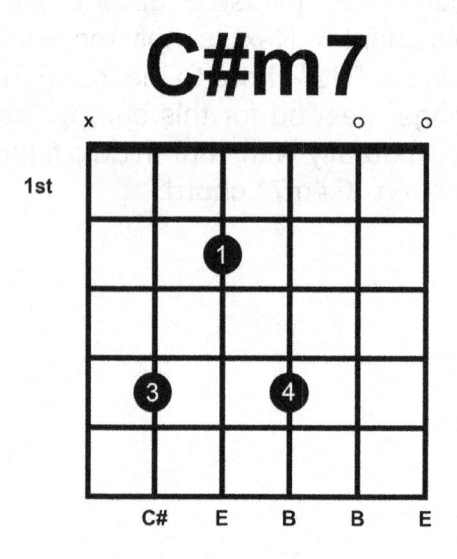

C#m7

(chord diagram: 1st fret; notes from low to high: x, C#, E, B, B, E; fingers 3, 1, 4)

While not technically built from the "B5" chord, this special "C#m7" is a related chord that you will need from time to time and especially playing in this open key of B. Begin by placing your ring finger (3) on the fourth fret of the fifth string [A]. Next, add your index finger (1) to the second fret of the fourth string [D]. Last, place your pinky finger (4) to the fourth fret of the third string [G]. Your middle finger (2) is not used in this chord. Strum the last five strings, beginning with the fifth string [A]. Note that the highest two strings, [B] and [e], will remain open. That is the key to making this chord sound open and full.

G, D and C Section Notes

What to know about the next three chapters

The next three chapters explore the use of the simple keys and chords of G, D and C. While there are some versions of these chords you may not have played before, the point of these are to learn *why* to use each one. These are especially helpful when deciding which capo placement to use. Each of these three place the tonic note of the scale at different intervals. The key of G places the tonic note at the top of the chord. For songs where the melody mainly is sung on the tonic note, this key is awesome! The key of D places the third note of the scale at the top. Again, if your melody is primarily a 3 then this key is best. The key of C places the fifth note of the scale at the top of many of your chords. Any songs primarily with a 5 in the melody work well with this key. Let's move on into this important material!

Chapter FIVE: "G5" and Related Chords

Understanding this chapter

Some of this chapter is definitely review for any seasoned guitar player, however, within it are several professional ways to play in the key of G that you may not use every day. Most of these chords are built with either the third frets of both the second [B] and first [e] strings pressed down or just the first [e] string. This keeps a consistent sound across all chords played. There is also a thumbed "D/F#" chord that everyone should know and use.

When using the key of G it is important to note that the benefits of the key lie in that the tonic note G is the last note played in the chord. When using this key the tonic note is struck in almost every chord and as the top note. Especially for songs where the melody is primarily on the root note, the key of G brings a ton of stability.

"G5" (Muting Fifth String)

Just about every guitarist learns how to play a "G" in week one of their learning. The more you play, the more you realize that you do not need to press down the fifth string [A] on the second fret. Muting that note turns the chord from a true "G" chord to a "G5". You have effectively muted the "B" note that was being played on the second fret of the fifth string [A]. In doing so, this new "G5" is a clearer sounding chord. The "B" note *muddies* the clarity of the "G". I use the "G5" just about any time that the "G" is necessary. So can you.

G5

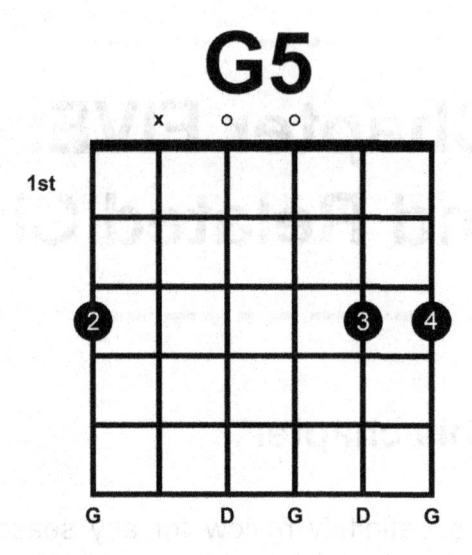

```
    x   o   o
1st
     |   |   |   |   |
     |   |   |   |   |
     2   |   |   3   4
     |   |   |   |   |
     |   |   |   |   |
     G   D   G   D   G
```

Just in case you need to see this chord spelled out, here is how you would build it step-by-step. Place your index finger (1) on the second fret of the fifth string [A]. This is the note you will mute by applying slight pressure to the string, but not enough to hear it sound. Follow with your middle finger (2) on the third fret of the sixth string [E]. Last, add your ring (3) and pinky fingers (4) to the third frets of both the second [B] and first [e] strings, respectively. Those final fingers should be tight fitting. Strum across all six strings and you will have a "G5" chord.

"Dsus"

Again, this is a fundamental chord that you may already know, but because it is so important I thought I would make sure everyone knows it. This is the 5 chord in the key of G.

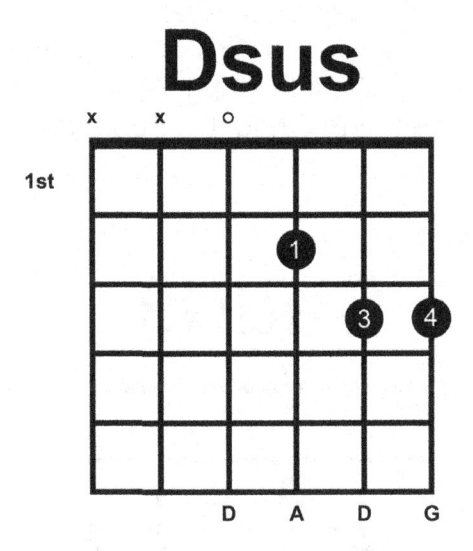

Dsus

Begin with your index finger (1) on the second fret of the third string [G]. Then add your ring finger (3) to the third fret of the second string [B]. The final step is to add your pinky finger (4) to the third fret of the first string [e]. Strum the last four strings. Note that to move from "G5" to "Dsus", you only need to move your middle finger (2) off the guitar and your index finger (1) to the second fret of the third string [G]. The transition is easy.

"Em7"

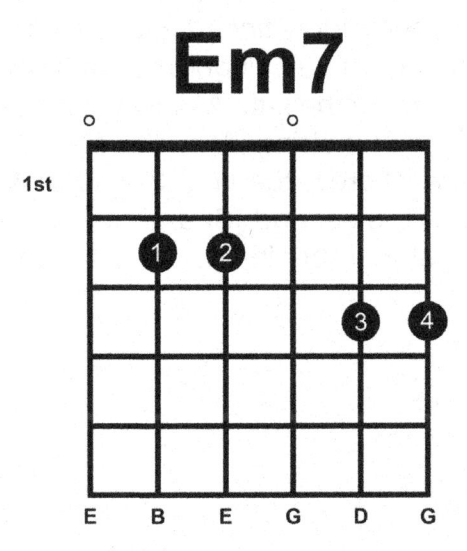

Em7

"Em7" is the 6m chord in the key of G. Keeping your ring (3) and pinky (4) fingers on the third frets of the second [B] and first [e] strings, add your index finger (1) to the second fret of the fifth string [A]. Last, add your middle finger (2) to the second fret of the fourth string [D]. Strum across all six strings.

"Cadd9"

Cadd9

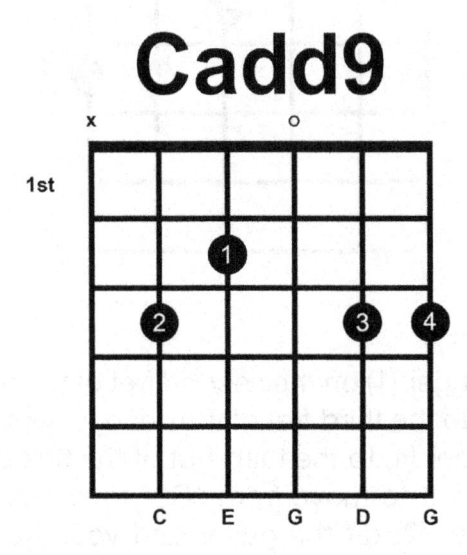

```
x       o
┌──┬──┬──┬──┬──┐
│  │  │  │  │  │  1st
├──┼──┼──┼──┼──┤
│  │  ①  │  │  │
├──┼──┼──┼──┼──┤
│  ②  │  │  ③  ④
├──┼──┼──┼──┼──┤
│  │  │  │  │  │
├──┼──┼──┼──┼──┤
│  │  │  │  │  │
└──┴──┴──┴──┴──┘
 C  E  G  D  G
```

"Cadd9" is about as popular as the "G" chord for most guitar players. It looks similar and is the 4 chord of the key of G. First, fret the "G5" we learned above. Next, move both your middle finger (2) and index finger (1) down one string each. This means your middle finger moves from the third fret of the sixth string [E] to the third fret of the fifth [A]. Likewise, the index finger moves from the second fret of the fifth string [A] to the second of the fourth string [D]. As in several of these chords, the ring (3) and pinky (4) fingers remain place on the third frets of the second [B] and first [e] strings, respectively. Strum only the last five strings beginning on the fifth string [A] to play a "Cadd9" chord.

"Am7"

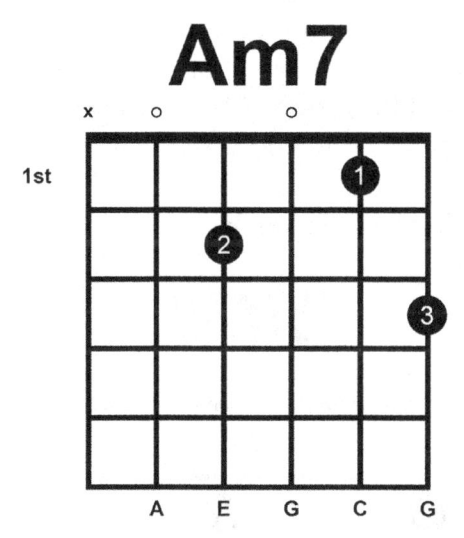

Am7

```
x  o     o
```
1st fret position, fingers: 1 on 2nd string 1st fret, 2 on 4th string 2nd fret, 3 on 1st string 3rd fret

Notes: A E G C G

The "Am7" is the 2m chord in the key of G. I recommend the "Am7" over the plain "Am" because of the third fret G note being played on the first string [e]. Here is how to build an "Am7" from scratch. First, place your index finger (1) on the first fret of the second string [B]. Then add your middle finger (2) to the second fret of the fourth string [D]. Last, add your ring finger (3) to the third fret of the first string [e]. Strum only the last five strings.

"G/B"

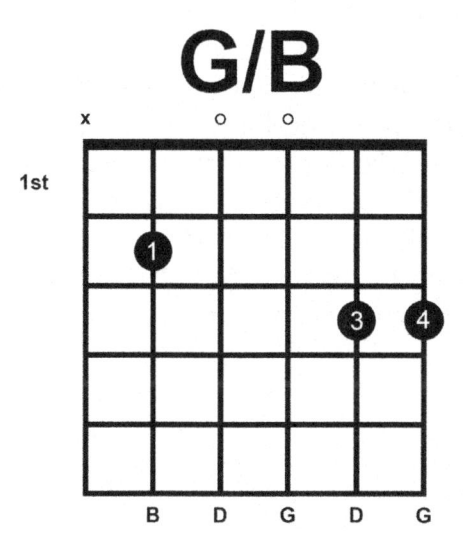

G/B

```
x     o  o
```
1st fret position, fingers: 1 on 5th string 2nd fret, 3 on 2nd string 3rd fret, 4 on 1st string 3rd fret

Notes: B D G D G

I include the "G/B" in this section because it can be used a lot. Any chord name over another is simply a chord with its root note shifted. In this case, the "G" chord has its root note shifted upward to B from G. To play a "G/B" chord, simply play a normal "G" chord (not "G5"), including the index finger on the second fret of the fifth string [A]. You then strum only the last five strings, omitting string six [E]. This chord has a lifting sound to it.

"D/F#" chord with the thumb

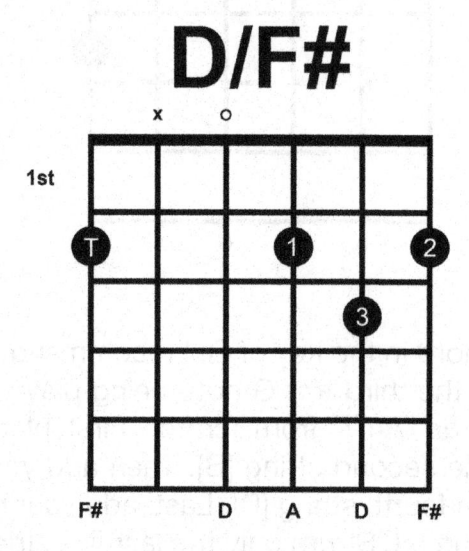

D/F#

The last chord for this series is the "D/F#" chord. This, too, is a normal chord with a shifted root note. In this case you need to add an "F#" note to the root, rather than taking away a note, like in the "G/B" chord. To play a "D/F#" fret a normal "D" chord, which is index finger (1) on the second fret of the fourth string [G]. Then add your ring finger (3) to the third fret of the second string [B] and then your middle finger (2) to the second fret of the first string [e]. Last, to form the "D/F#" you need to apply your thumb (T) to the second fret of the sixth string [E]. You may strum all six strings, however I recommend slightly muting the fifth string "A". This allows the F# note to cut through the mix of the chord being played.

Chapter SIX: "D" and Related Chords

Understanding this chapter

As in the chapter about playing in the key of G, this chapter has some review chords in it. That being noted, I have intentionally laid out a few alternative ways to play these familiar chords that I use more often now than the traditional methods. Give them a shot. You never know when you may want to use them.

While the key of G has the root note as the top note of many of the chords, the key of D has the third note of the scale on top. This is especially great for songs with melodies primarily singing the third note of the scale.

"D"

D

x x o

1st

1 — 1
3

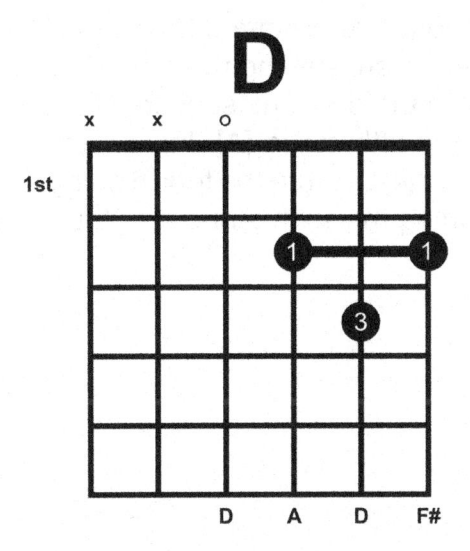

D A D F#

Traditionally, a "D" chord uses the index (1), ring (3) and middle (2) fingers. From time to time it can be helpful to barre the second frets of the third [G] through first [e] strings with the index finger (1). This lets you fret the chord faster and move to chords, like "D/C#" more easily. Begin by barring your index finger (1) on to the second frets of the third [G], second [B] and first [e] strings. Last, add your ring finger (3) to the third fret of the second string [B]. Strum only the last four strings.

"D/C#"

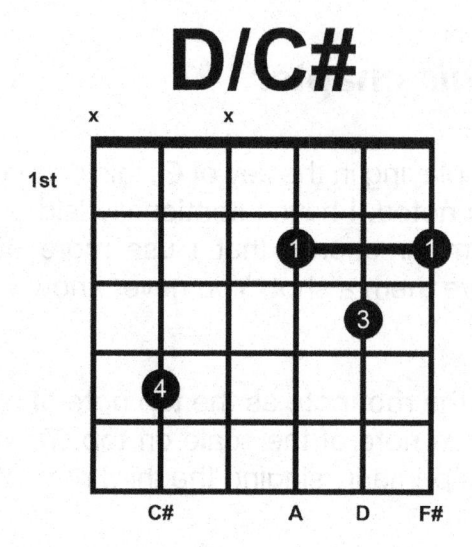

The "D/C#" is another chord over a shifted bass note like the previous "G/B" you learned. In this case, we are shifting the bass note D down to a C#. First, build your "D" chord from the previous section. Next, add your pinky finger (4) to the fourth fret of the fifth string [A]. Initially this may be a stretch for you. Allow that pinky finger (4) to mute the fourth string [D]. Strum now across the last five strings, omitting the sixth string [E]. You have built a "D/C#".

"Bm11" (A special and unconventional way...)

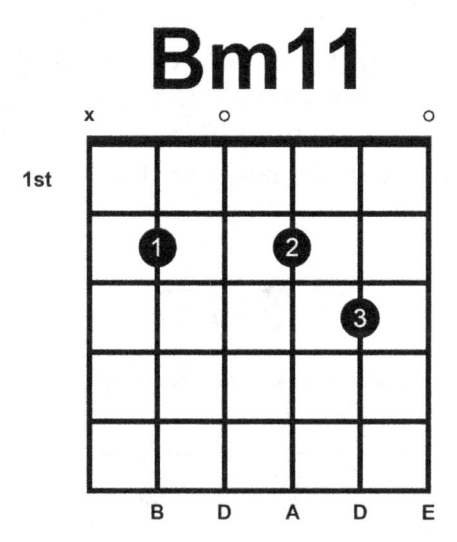

Bm11

```
    x    o         o
1st ┌──┬──┬──┬──┬──┐
    │  │  │  │  │  │
    ├──┼──┼──┼──┼──┤
    │  │①│  │②│  │
    ├──┼──┼──┼──┼──┤
    │  │  │  │  │③│
    ├──┼──┼──┼──┼──┤
    │  │  │  │  │  │
    ├──┼──┼──┼──┼──┤
    │  │  │  │  │  │
    └──┴──┴──┴──┴──┘
     B  D  A  D  E
```

Moving on down the scale we arrive at a very special "Bm11" chord. Most play a "Bm" and "Bm7" using the barre chord version, barring the second fret. In this version, I demonstrate an easier way to play the chord and a faster way to transition to and from it from chords like "D" and "Asus". It is an 11 chord because of the open E note from the top string. Do not let this confuse you, it can be used instead of a true "Bm" or "Bm7" chord.

To build this newer "Bm11" begin by placing your index finger (1) on the second fret of the fifth string [A]. Next, add you middle finger (2) to the second fret of the third string [G]. Last, place your ring finger (3) on the third fret of the second string [B]. Strum only the last five strings. Strings four [D] and one [e] need to remain open. This is an easy "Bm11". Interestingly, simply strum the last four strings of the "Bm11" to play a "D2". Or, move your middle finger (2) to the second fret of the first string [e] and your index finger (1) to the second fret of the third string [G] to form a full "D" chord. Transitioning to and from "D" to "Bm11" is now simple.

"Asus" (Barring version)

The "Asus" chord (or the 5 chord in the key of D) is simple to get to after you have built our last "Bm11". You simply need to move your index finger (1) from the second fret of the fifth string [A] to the second fret of the fourth string [D] and now strum across the last five strings. This makes an "Asus".

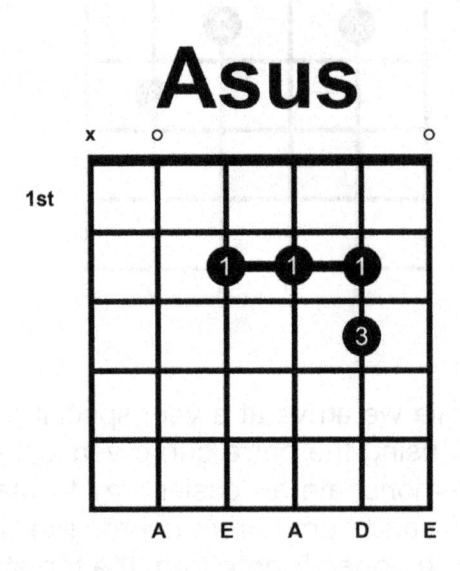

Asus

An alternative way to play an "Asus" that I use most often is to play the same chord, but as a barre version. Initially this may sound more difficult, but as you learn the barre version of "Asus" you may find it more useful. To begin, barre the second frets of both the fourth [D] and the third [G] strings with your index finger (1). Last, add your ring finger (3) to the third fret of the second string [B]. Strum the last five strings. This chord transitions easily to a barred "A" chord by simply releasing your ring finger (3) and barring across the second fret of the [B] string with the index finger (1) (that is already barring the two preceding strings). Make sure that you leave open the first string [e]. This may be difficult at first, but practice makes this one perfect.

"G2"

G2

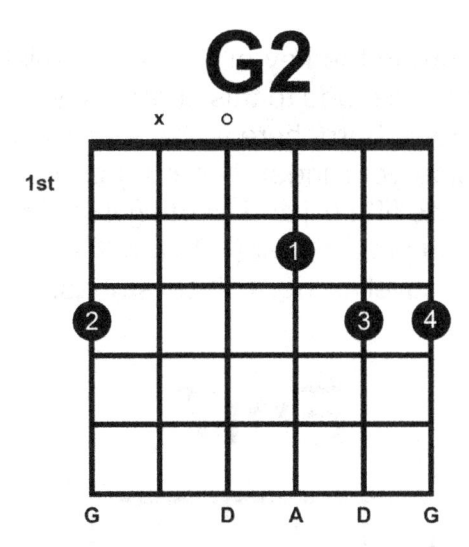

```
x   o
```
1st

G D A D G

Many of us learn "G" during lesson one of guitar. In the previous chapter we discovered the "G5" chord. While playing in the key of D, the "G2" is valuable. The "G2" is the 4 chord in the key of D. If you are newer to playing or just missed this one, it is pretty awesome. Here is how to play a "G2" chord. First, begin by building your "G5" chord learned in the previous chapter. In case you are skipping around this is how to do that: Place your index finger (1) on the second fret of the fifth string [A]. This is the note you will mute by applying slight pressure to the string, but not enough to hear it sound. Follow with your middle finger (2) on the third fret of the sixth string [E]. Last, add your ring (3) and pinky fingers (4) to the third frets of both the second [B] and first [e] strings, respectively.

From the "G5" chord, move your index finger (1) from the second fret of the fifth string [A] and move it over to the second fret of the third string [G]. While in the "G5" you were using the index finger (1) to mute a string, this time you need to firmly press that second fret of the third string [G] down. You still need to mute the fifth string [A]. Do so by allowing your middle finger (2) to remain firmly on the third fret of the sixth string [E] and gently muting the fifth string [A]. Strum across all six strings, muting the fifth [A] to form a "G2" chord.

"Em7" (A special barre version)

The "Em7" is the 2m chord in the key of D. While a relatively easy chord to play, one modification can be made to this chord as we will see. First, in case you have never learned this chord, here is the step-by-step directions to do that: You begin by placing your index finger (1) and your middle finger (2) onto the second frets of the fifth [A] and fourth [D] strings respectively. Next, add your ring finger (3) and pinky finger (4) to the third frets of the second [B] and first [e] strings, respectively. Strum all six strings.

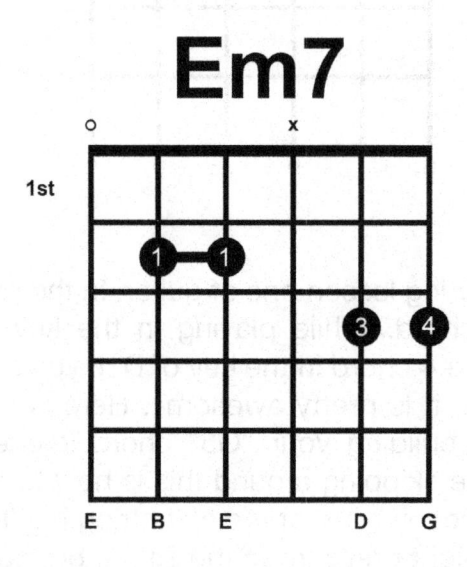

The modification that I make to this is to play the fifth string [A] with the index finger (1) on the second fret and allow that same finger to barre the second fret of the fourth string [A]. Strum all six strings. The key to this is that it frees up the middle finger (2) for quick transitioning for chords like "G", "Cadd9" and others.

Chapter SEVEN: "C" and Related Chords

Understanding this chapter

The key of C is useful when playing open chords, especially with a capo. You will notice as we move throughout these chords that we keep the fifth note [G] in the scale of C at the top of the chord. As opposed to the key of D where the third note in the scale remains at the top, or the key of G where the first note, or tonic note, remains at the top of the chord. Depending on how the song you are playing is written, having the fifth note may be perfect.

"C" (Keeping pinky (4) on the third fret of the first string [e] throughout as much as possible)

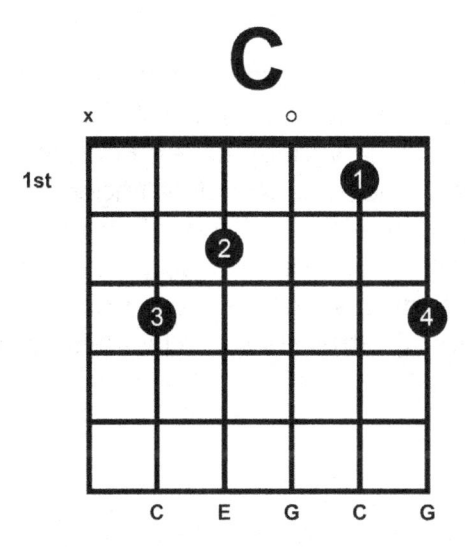

C

```
    x           o
1st ┌─┬─┬─┬─┬─┐
    │ │ │ │①│
    ├─┼─┼─┼─┼─┤
    │ │②│ │ │
    ├─┼─┼─┼─┼─┤
    │③│ │ │④│
    ├─┼─┼─┼─┼─┤
    │ │ │ │ │
    ├─┼─┼─┼─┼─┤
    │ │ │ │ │
    └─┴─┴─┴─┴─┘
     C E G C G
```

To begin in the key of C we have to learn the fundamental version of the "C" chord that makes this key awesome. The power is in the pinky [end Tweet].

First, build a normal "C" chord. Just in case you need to know how to do that, here is the process: Begin by placing the index finger (1) on the first fret of the second string [B]. Next, add your middle finger (2) to the second fret of the fourth string [D]. Finally, add your ring finger (3) to the third fret of the fifth string [A]. The bonus note to add to the standard "C" chord is the pinky finger (4) to the third fret of the first string [e]. Strum across the last five strings to form a "C" chord with the added pinky.

"C/B" (Including the pinky (4))

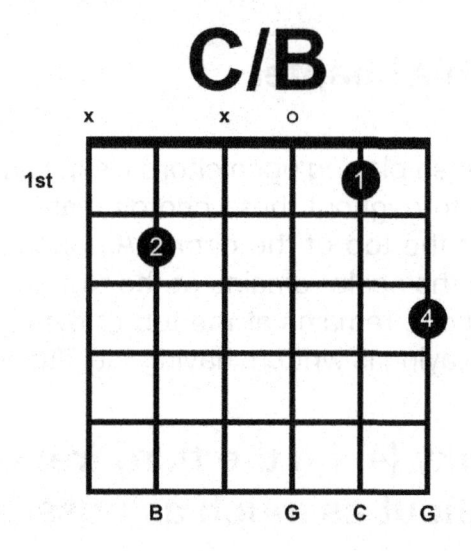

The next few chords descend down the C scale. To begin that descent, let me show you a very easy transition to the "C/B" chord. This chord can be used to replace a "G" chord at various times. First, fret the "C" chord from the previous section. Next, move your middle finger (2) from the second fret of the fourth string [D] to the second fret of the fifth string [A]. You are removing your ring finger (3) altogether. Use your middle finger (2) to mute the fourth string [D] by adding slight pressure borrowed from the pressure needed for the fifth string [A]. Strum only the last five strings, just like the "C" chord.

"Am7"

Am7

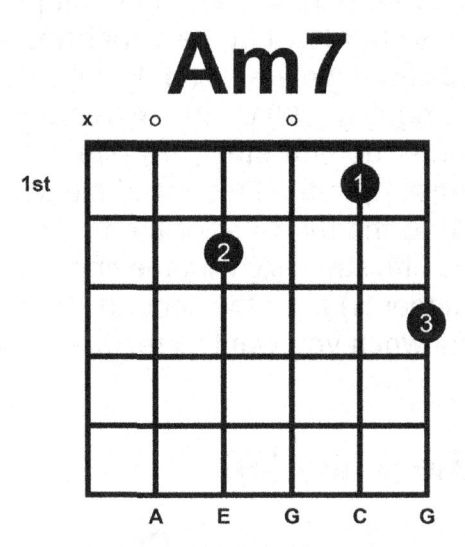

The next chord is probably one you have been playing for a while. The only detail I would add is that when playing an "Am7" using this key of C style, always include your pinky (4) to the third fret of the first string [e]. In case you are looking to build this chord from the ground up, here is the process: First, place your index finger (1) on the first fret of the second string [B]. Then add your middle finger (2) to the second fret of the fourth string [D]. Last, add your pinky finger (4) to the third fret of the first string [e]. Strum only the last five strings.

"Gsus" (Using the pinky (4))

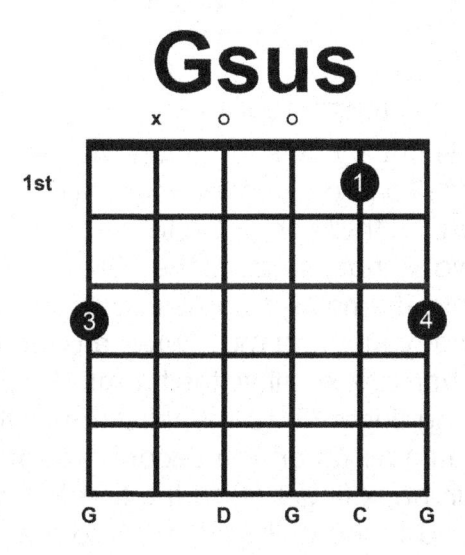

Gsus

Now we build a special 5 chord in the key of C. The "Gsus" chord is somehow overlooked in basic guitar instruction, but professionals use it all the time. The power in this chord is that the upper two strings are the same notes as the dominant C chord we are using. Here is how to build a "Gsus" chord: First, place your ring finger (3) on the third fret of the sixth string [E]. Let that finger gently mute the fifth string [A] directly beside the sixth [E]. Next, add your index finger (1) to the first fret of the second string [B]. Last, add your pinky finger (4) to the third fret of the first string [e]. Strum all six strings (having muted the fifth string [A] with the ring finger (3)). Note that you can release your index finger (1) from the second string [B] to form an open "G" chord. This is helpful when you want to resolve your "Gsus" chord to a "G".

"Fadd9" (Using the pinky (4))

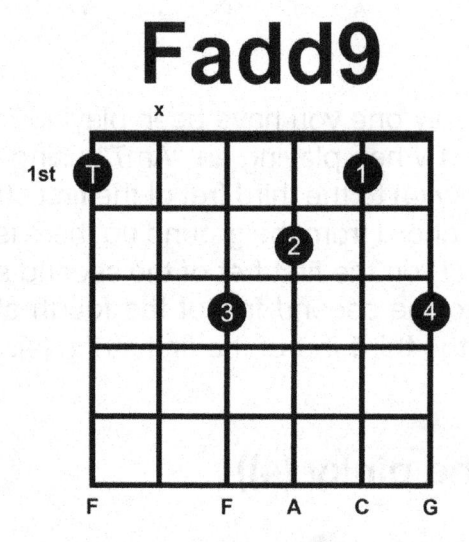

Fadd9

The 4 chord in the key of C is "F". While you may play a normal "F" chord, as far as this book that is not a whole lot of fun. We need to play something a little shinier. The "Fadd9" chord using the thumb (T) is one that I play more often in the key of C than the traditional "F". In the same way that the "Gsus" uses the same upper two strings, so does the "Fadd9". Here is how to build that chord: First, use your thumb (T) to press down the first fret of the sixth string [E]. This means that your hand must wrap around the neck more than when playing a typical chord. Next, allow the thumb (T) to mute the fifth string [A]. Then you add the ring finger (3) to the third fret of the fourth string [D]. Next, place your middle finger (2) on the second fret of the third string [G]. Continuing on, add your index finger (1) to the first fret of the second string [B]. Last, but not least, add your pinky finger (4) to the third fret of the first string [e]. Strum across all six strings to form a thumbed "Fadd9".

"C/E"

C/E

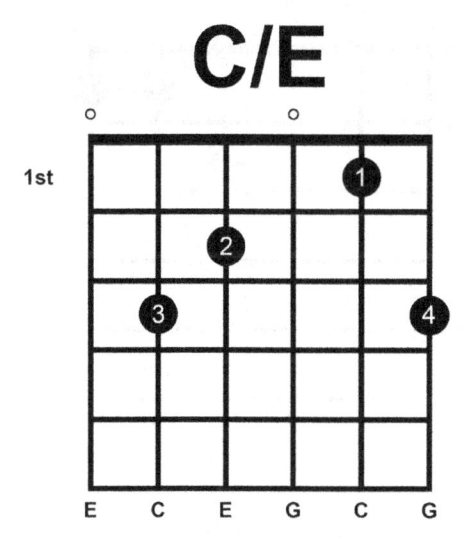

```
   o        o
1st
         ①
      ②
   ③        ④


E  C  E  G  C  G
```

It is important to quickly note that from time to time you will need to use the chord over shifted bass note chord "C/E". To do so, form your "C" chord learned at the beginning of this chapter, but instead of strumming only the bottom five strings, strum all six, including the low sixth string [E]. That sixth string [E] note is the shifted bass note of E making this the "C/E" chord.

"Dm7"

Dm7

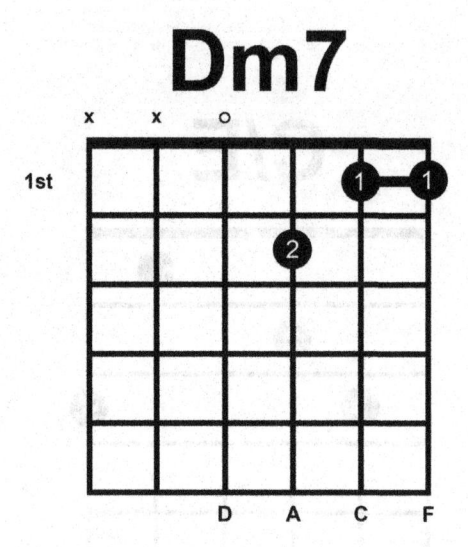

The final chord to note in the key of C is the 2m chord. You could play a normal "Dm" chord and it work as the 2m, but what fun is that? I typically play the "Dm7" because it employs a C note that is not found in the "Dm" chord. Since we are in the key of C, that extra C note continues the continuity found in this key. Here is how to build a "Dm7". First, place your middle finger (2) on the second fret of the third string [G]. Last, barre the first frets of both the second [B] and first [e] strings with your index finger (1). Strum the last four strings to play a "Dm7" chord.

Chapter EIGHT: Strange But Cool Chords

The following chords do not have a proper place, but I use them often and they are really cool.

The following chords are not part of a particular key, but are still incredible and worth learning. This is especially so of the first chord, the moveable "D".

Moveable "D"

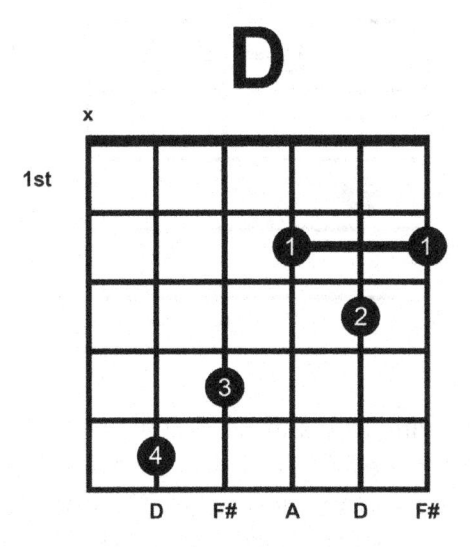

D

```
x
    1st
         ●——●   (1)
            ●    (2)
         ●       (3)
       ●         (4)
       D  F# A  D  F#
```

I learned this chord when I was in college. The moveable "D" chord is a basic "C" chord that is barred on the second fret and able to move anywhere up and down the neck. Initially this chord is tough to play, but becomes easier with practice. Here is how to build it and some ways to use it: First, barre across the second frets of the third [G], second [B] and first [e] strings, respectively. Next, add your middle finger (2) to the third fret of the second string [B]. Continue by adding your ring finger (3) to the fourth fret of the fourth string [D]. Finally, stretch your pinky finger (4) all the way across to the fifth fret of the fifth string [A]. Yes, when you first build this chord, it may seem impossible. You can make this work, you just need to practice it. Strum only the last five strings, omitting the bottom [E] string.

You have built a moveable "D" chord. If you move each of your fingers down one fret you are building a "D♭" or "C#" chord. Move everything up from the "D" position by one fret and you build an "E♭" or "D#". Up two frets and you have an "E" chord. Up three frets and you have an "F" chord. Moving up and down the neck will produce as many major chords as your guitar neck will allow. In essence, learning this one chord position adds between twelve and fifteen chords to your repertoire. Amazing!

"A/C#"

A/C#

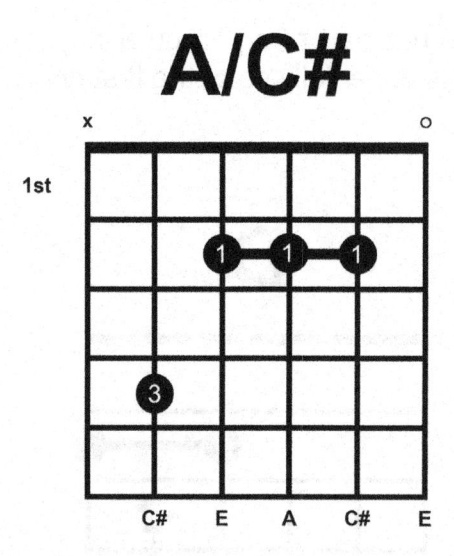

"A/C#" is an "A" chord with the shifted bass note of "C#". This chord is helpful when playing in the key of A and transitions well to the "D" chord. First we need to build a barred version of an "A" chord. To do so, use your index finger (1) to barre across the fourth [D], third [G] and second [B] strings on the second frets. You need to leave the first string [e] open. Last, place your ring finger (3) on the fourth fret of the fifth string [A]. Strum the last five strings. Note that this chord transitions to the standard "D" chord well, but it also is primed to transition to the moveable "D" that you learned at the beginning of this chapter.

"E/G#"

E/G#

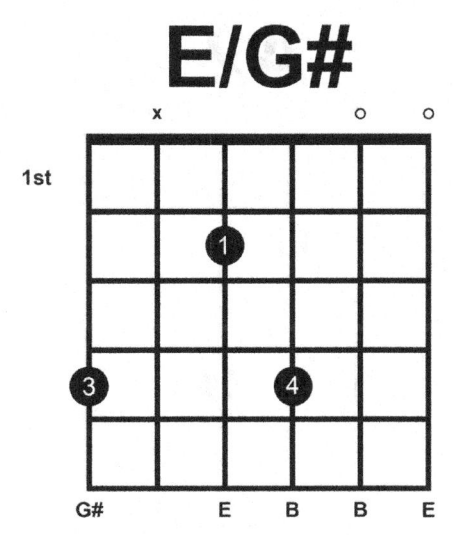

[Chord diagram: 1st fret position. X on 5th string, open on 2nd and 1st strings. Finger 1 on 2nd fret of 4th string, finger 3 on 4th fret of 6th string, finger 4 on 4th fret of 3rd string. Notes from low to high: G#, E, B, B, E.]

The "E/G#" is a critical chord when playing in the open key of E. The "E/G#" is the "E" chord with a shifted bass note of "G#". It transitions well to the "A2" chord. To build the "E/G#" first place your ring finger (3) on the fourth fret of the sixth string [E]. Allow that finger to mute the fifth string [A] by lightly resting on it as you are pressing down the sixth string [E]. Next, add your index finger (1) to the second fret of the fourth string [D]. Last, add your pinky finger (4) to the fourth fret of the third string [G]. Strum across all six strings.

As an aside, you may use the "E/G#" as a moveable chord, but do not strum across all six strings. You have three strings pressed down for the "E/G#", if you move that chord up two frets and strum only the strings you have pressed down then you have built an "F#/A#". Note, you cannot play the open strings for these moveable versions like you did with the "E/G#". Move the chord up one more set of frets and you have built a "G/B".

"A2"

A2

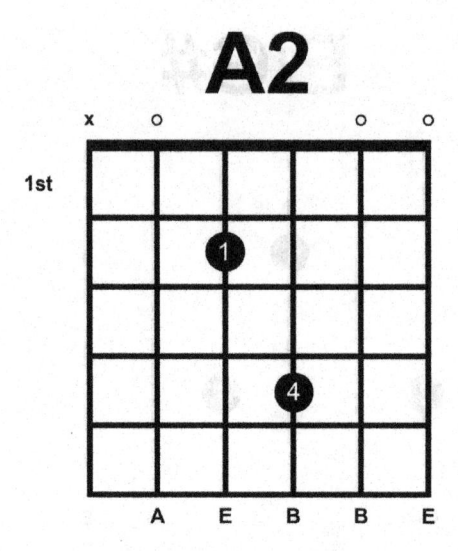

```
x  o        o  o
┌──┬──┬──┬──┬──┐
1st
├──┼──┼──┼──┼──┤
│  │  │ 1│  │  │
├──┼──┼──┼──┼──┤
├──┼──┼──┼──┼──┤
│  │  │  │ 4│  │
├──┼──┼──┼──┼──┤
└──┴──┴──┴──┴──┘
 A  E  B  B  E
```

From the "E/G#" built in the last section, remove your muting of the fifth string [A] and strum only the last five strings to play a special "A2" chord. As you imagine, the "E/G#" and this "A2" are played quite often.

"E2"

E2

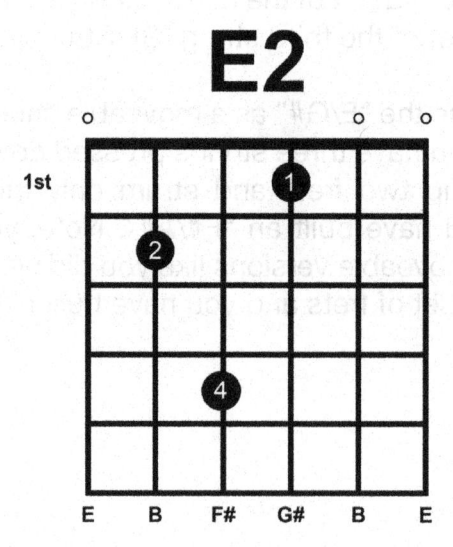

```
o     o  o
┌──┬──┬──┬──┬──┐
1st         │ 1│
├──┼──┼──┼──┼──┤
│  │ 2│  │  │  │
├──┼──┼──┼──┼──┤
├──┼──┼──┼──┼──┤
│  │  │ 4│  │  │
├──┼──┼──┼──┼──┤
└──┴──┴──┴──┴──┘
 E  B  F# G# B  E
```

The next chord "E2" is just a cool sounding chord. It does not belong to any particular pattern of chords in this book, but it still worth giving a try. First, place your middle finger (2) on the second fret of the fifth string [A]. Next, add your pinky finger (4) to the fourth string [D]. Last, place your index finger (1) on the first fret of the third string [G]. Strum across all six strings. This chord may take time as the stretch of the pinky (4) and the index (1) fingers are typically not used to making such a stretch. This chord is beautiful and rich.

"A2"

A2

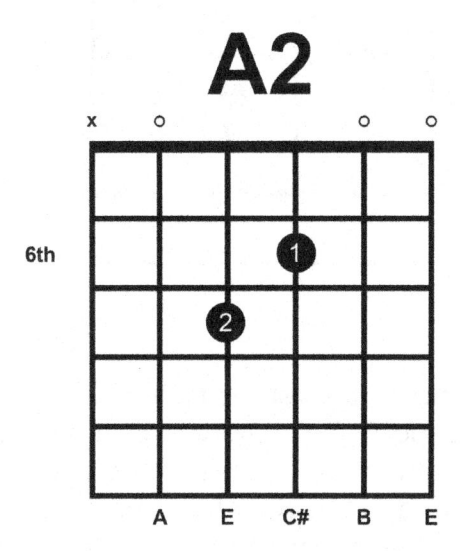

```
x    o         o    o
```

6th

A   E   C#   B   E

This special "A2" chord is not one you will use all the time, but is very helpful when coming from a high "E5" chord or if you just want to dazzle your friends with a special chord. First, place your middle finger (2) onto the seventh fret of the fourth string [D]. Last, add your index finger (1) to the sixth fret of the third string [G]. Strum only the last five strings.

"D2" or "Dadd9"

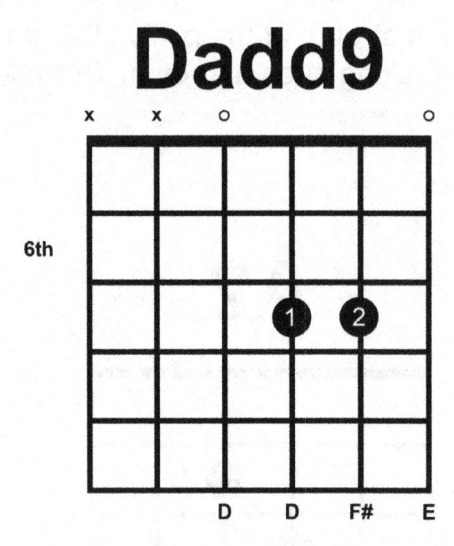

Dadd9

The final chord in this chapter is a very special "D2". In fact, this chord may better be known as a "Dadd9". This chord transitions well to and from the previous "A2" you just learned. To build it, place your index finger (1) onto the seventh fret of the third string [G] and your middle finger (2) onto the seventh fret of the second string [B]. Strum only the last four strings. This chord is not always practical to get to, but is gorgeous.

Practical Application Sections

The set up for head math, capos, tunings, and the rest of this book...

The last half of this book is about music theory and secrets in how to memorize music easily. We will walk through some awesome ways to use your guitar capo. We look over several types of guitar picks and how to use them and much more. You can use many of the new chords you learned in the first half of this book now to employ them while learning music theory and more in the last half of this book.

Before you begin, know that you can learn this material. If you have trouble understanding any of these sections please send me an email at micah@micahbrooks.com. My goal in writing this book is to help you grow as a musician. Please let me help if you need it.

Chapter NINE: Head Math (How To Use Numbers)

Music is math

This section is devoted to music theory. However, before you turn the page, my aim is to give you the most applicable section of music theory that you will ever need. There will be no mention of accidentals or words like harmonic progression. Rather, I want to do my best to train you in practical music theory you can use every time you play guitar. I use this stuff every moment I pick up my guitar and so can you. Please know that you can understand these concepts.

One more disclaimer, the method I propose next is basic. If you have music theory friends, they may either say "duh" or attempt to clutter this with more information. These are the basic building blocks for theory that all musicians need. This is not a comprehensive study. To do that, go to Belmont University in Nashville, TN where I went or another music school. They know it all there. This is for those of us in the trenches. This is for anyone who wants the basics so that you can get out there and perform.

Numbers

Music is built on notes. Notes join in series to create scales. The fundamental or root note of the scale is the tonic note. A chord is the addition of two or more notes played at the same time. Playing in a certain key means that you are playing music by the rules of particularly predefined tones that work well with one another. Every key has a fundamental or root chord. This is the **1 chord**. The 1 chord is the foundation for the other chords coming next in what I will call the *chord scale*.

There is a more in depth section below explaining what is under the hood of each of the following chords. This is a bird's eye perspective for understanding how chords relate to one another. If you can understand this section then you will be able to hear and play just about any pop or worship song you want.

Building from the 1 chord we spoke about above, the 4 and 5 chords relate most solidly with the 1 chord. Because this is a guitar book, let me use the key of G as an example throughout the rest of this section. It will help if you play these chords while you read along to hear the differences mentioned. In the key of G, the 1 chord is "G". You guessed it! The 4 chord is the "C" chord and the 5 chord is "D". These three numbers are the three pillar chords in any key that are like the structural triangle that all the others derive. While the 1 chord is dominant, the 4 and 5 are also supremely dominant chords in any key.

Next, the 2m and the 6m chords derive from the 4 and 1 chords, respectively. In fact, a 2m7 and 6m7 are simply 4 and 1 chords with their bass notes shifted down the scale two notes. In the key of G, the 2m chord is an "Am" and the 6m is an "Em". If you have played much in the key of G then you know how important these two chords are to most songs.

Moving forward, music theory would say that the 3m and 7dim are the final chords you should learn when learning these types of major chord scales. Practically though, you will rarely play a 3m or 7dim. Especially in popular music. Instead, I recommend learning the 1/3 and 5/7 chords. These are chords with shifted up bass notes, by the amount of two steps, from both the 1 chord and the 5 chord. In the case of the key of G these chords would be 1/3 = "G/B" and the 5/7 = "D/F#". I imagine that you have seen these chords before. They are foundational.

There are some outlier chords that we need to discuss before diving into the finer details. The ♭7 and the 2-Major chords are standard, but not obvious forms of any chord scale. The ♭7 chord assumes an entirely flattened step down from the tonic chord, whereas music theory says that the seventh note in the scale is not a whole-step, but merely a half-step. In the key of G this ♭7 chord is an "F". The 2-Major chord is also an outlier. While more rare than the b7, you can come across one. The 2-Major assumes that instead of playing a 2m chord (like "Am" in the key of G) you play a 2-Major (which would be "A" in the key of G). This trick is used in country music a lot and in ancient hymn writing.

Basic chord theory - Let's drill this down

I am going to drill down into each chord number and how each triad is built. I will do my best not to lose you, rather I hope to give you insight into being able to see chord relationships and how each interacts with one another. The goal is for you to be a better guitarist. Knowing this stuff will increase that likelihood.

Each of these little sections assumes we are building from the foundational 1 chord. Music theorists can, and some will, make this more complicated. Do your best to stay focused and use the key of G examples throughout.

1 Chord

The 1 chord, as noted before, is foundational and fundamental. It is the chord that we will reference most of the others chords to. It is like the President of the United States. Sure, the Vice President is important, but less so than the President. The 1 chord is built on the triad of 1, 3 and 5 notes in the major scale. Please understand that all throughout the rest of this chapter, we now assume a major scale. There are several other scales we could use, but for popular music, the major scale is the most played. In the key of G, the 1 chord is the "G" chord and is built using the notes G, B and D. You can rearrange those letters however you would like (called inversions) and you will still have a "G" chord.

4 Chord

The 4 chord shares one very important note with the 1 chord, which is the root note G. A 4 chord, using the same scale as from the 1 chord is built as 1, 4, 6. The root position for this chord, however, would really be 4, 6 and 1. The 4 being the root note of the 4 chord. In the key of G example, the 4 chord is a "C" chord and is built C, E and G. Thus, the G note (which is the tonic note of the G scale) is shared between these two chords. This helps them to be related musically.

5 Chord

The 5 chord shares one important note with the 1 chord, like the 4 did, but this time it is the 5 note, rather than the 1. This makes this chord have almost an opposing sound to the 1 chord. Whereas the 4 chord sounds more complimentary. A 5 chord is built as 5, 7, 2. 5 is the root note of this chord.

In the key of G, this is the "D" chord and these notes would be D, F# and A. Again, rearrange those notes however you would like and you still have a "D" chord.

2m Chord

The 2m chord is interestingly a 4 chord with the bass note shifted down two steps. Technically the 2m7 is the 4 chord shifted, but the purpose is the same. A 2m chord is built as the 2, 4 and 6 notes in the scale. Remember, a 4 chord is a 1, 4 and 6. The 2m chord in the key of G is "Am". The notes are A, C and E.

6m Chord

The 6m chord is one used in just about every pop song. It is as famous as the 1, 4 and 5 chords. Like the 2m, the 6m is a derivative of an important chord. The 6m and the 1 chord are almost the same. In fact, a 6m7 is made of the same notes as a 1 chord, but the bass note is shifted downward two steps. In the key of G the "Em" is the 6m. If you have played much in the key of G then you have definitely played an "Em". Those notes are E, G and B.

3m Chord

Before I go into the 1/3 chord, which I believe is more useful when performing using numbers, I do want to explain the more traditional 3m. The 3m, like the other minors, is a 5 chord with a shifted down bass note of two steps (again, technically this is a true 3m7, not the 3m). This chord has a dark feeling when played in pop music. It is used, but it is rare. The notes are 3, 5 and 7. For the key of G, these notes are E, G and B. The chord in the key of G is a "Bm".

7dim Chord

The 7dim (or diminished or the degrees symbol "°") chord is about as rare today as you can imagine. While this was not so twenty or thirty years ago, the 5/7 chord has mainly taken its place. Diminished chords are utterly dark and normally passing chords, meaning most players do not stay on them long. The notes are 7, 2 and 4. You will notice that the note 4 is particularly drab. In the key of G these notes are F#, A and C. The chord is an "F#dim". Note that these notes are the same as a 5^7 chord, but without the 5 bass note. In the key of G it would be a D7 chord, with the bass note being an F#. This is useful in building this chord quickly if you needed to.

1/3 Chord

Instead of the 3m, in popular music we play a 1/3. This is simpler and sounds smoother. A 1/3 is just as it sounds: a full 1 chord with this bass note shifted up to a 3 note. The one chord being a 1, 3 and 5 and then the shifted bass note being a 3. In the key of G this chord is a "G/B". Those notes are B, D and G. This chord has a sense of movement to it. What that means is that typically you will play this chord on the way to the next one. Whereas with a 1, 4 or 5 chord you may rest measures or most of a verse/chorus on one of those chords. I cannot think of a time where I spent more than one or two measures on a 1/3. It has the sense of transition or motion to it.

5/7 Chord

Extremely similar to the 1/3, the 5/7 chord is simply a 5 chord with a shifted up 7 note in the bass. Another transition chord, these notes are 7, 2 and 5. In the key of G this is a "D/F#" chord and is built F#, A and D. This chord is used often to transition from the 1 chord ("G") to the 6m chord ("Em").

♭7 Chord

Music has rules that are meant to be broken. It would be a terrible dictator. The ♭7 (flat seven) chord is used quite a bit, but one of the notes lies outside the major scale. The ♭7 chord employs the ♭7 note in the major scale as its foundation. Typically the major seventh note is used, however in certain cases, the ♭7 is used. The ♭7 chord is built as ♭7, 2 and 4. Notice the 2 and 4. These notes give the chord stability in the major scale we are in. The ♭7 note is the outlier. In the key of G the "F" chord is the ♭7. Those notes are F, A and C. If you play the chords "G", then "C", "D" and then play an "F" chord you will hear the properties of the ♭7. It sounds both right and wrong in one motion. Music is awesome!

2-Major Chord

Similar to the ♭7 chord, the 2-Major chord has one note that does not belong in the laws of the scale yet still works to our ears. The 2-Major chord is built on, you guessed it, the 2 chord being major, rather than minor. Typically you will see the 2m chord played. The 2-Major assumes these notes: 2, #4 (sharp 4) and 6. Remember, the 2m was a 2, 4 and 6. That #4 note brings a whole new character to a song. In the key of G the 2-Major chord is "A". Those notes are A, C# and E. This chord may be an integral part of a song when it is used, but most of the time it is to catch the surprise of the listener. I feel like I have heard it mostly at the end of bridges, but before a final chorus, just to make the song more interesting.

How to memorize your songs for the stage and hear every song on the radio in numbers...

When you begin to hear in numbers and not just chords in a key, you will be able to stand on stage, for the most part, without any notes, charts or sheet music. This all comes with familiarity of knowing what each chord and number sounds like. A 1 chord is distinctly different from a 4 or a 5. A 6m and a 2m sound very different, even though they are both minor chords. It takes a fair amount of practice, but at some particular moment it becomes second nature. I am going to give you an overview of how I think of each chord. It may be that other teachers teach this in a different manner, however the principles will be the same no matter what. We are all working with the same set of fundamental rules.

Please make sure you have read the section above and that you understand what each of these sets of numbers consists of before diving into this section. Those ideas are foundational to the ones we are about to go over. Now onward!

Hearing a 1 chord

The 1 chord is the foundational chord. I keep saying that. All others jettison off of it. Once you establish aurally the 1 chord you can then figure out all the others. If you have trouble distinguishing it from the others, then you are not ready to work with numbers. You should be able to *hear* a 1 chord and know what it is. Here is an example that we will continue through this section: play a standard G chord. This will be our 1 chord example throughout the rest of this chapter.

Hearing a 4 chord

The 4 chord always sounds like it wants to resolve or fall back to a 1 chord. The only note that it shares with the 1 chord is the tonic note (or the 1 note in the scale), yet to the ear it always sounds incomplete. In hearing a 4 it wants to revert back to a 1 chord. If you are familiar with hymns, the "Amen" at the end of "The Doxology" is a 4 chord that settles into a 1 chord. The 4 chord in the key of G is the "C" chord. Play a "C" chord and then let it resolve back to the 1 chord "G". You should notice a sort of settling sound.

Hearing a 5 chord

A 5 chord is its own animal. It shares the 5 note with the 1 chord, but the 5 chord is in itself pretty dominant. In fact, in music theory, the 5 chord is called the dominant fifth. In my observance the 5 chord is a springboard back to the 1 chord. It will go there easily, but is itself it's own chord. A 5 also transitions smoothly to a 4 chord. Play a "D" chord then move to the "G" chord. You will hear the important nature of the "D" feeling like a good transition to the "G". That is the 5 moving to a 1. Do the reverse. Play a "G" to a "D". This time you will hear the sound of two chords interacting well together. However, if you end a song using the 5 chord it would almost certainly feel unresolved. Now play a "D" (5) to a "C" (4) chord. This progression has a very distinct sound. It is as if the 5 chord, while being dominant, wanted to get to a 4 chord. The 5 chord causes musical angst while the 4 chord is more settling. Knowing what you are playing using numbers will better your ability to memorize music.

Hearing a 6m chord

A 6m chord is a 1 chord with the bass note shifted down. That concept was explained earlier. The 6m chord is a minor chord. Minor chords have a darker sound than brighter major chords. In my opinion, the 6m is the darkest. Most pop songs utilize at least one 6m. In the key of G the 6m chord is "Em". Switching from "G" to "Em" you will hear the transition from the more cheerful major chord (1 chord) to the darker minor chord (6m).

Hearing a 2m chord

A 2m chord is also a minor chord, but I find it to be a little brighter (for a minor chord) than the 6m. In fact, some have said that the 2m is the new 5. What that means is that some songwriters have abandoned using the 5 chord in lieu of a 2m. The 2m in the key of G is "Am". Moving from 1 to 2m has a sense of lifting. Move a 1 to 2m and then to 4 and you will sense moving up the scale. Play a "G" chord to an "Am" and then the "C" chord.

Distinguishing between a 2m and a 6m can be difficult at first. I find the 6m to be dark, while the 2m sounds lighter. Practice playing between a "G" to "Em" and then "G" to "Am". You should begin to hear the difference and be able to determine the 6m from the 2m in other keys as well.

Hearing a 1/3 and 5/7 chord

The 1/3 and 5/7 chords are each standard 1 and 5 chords, but with shifted bass notes. If you are beginning to hear a definite 1 and 5 chord, then the shifted bass note will not throw you off. The 1/3 and 5/7 each have a *passing chord* sense to them. What this means is that they are not chords you stay on long. Rather, you will use these to move from a more stable chord, like a 1, 4 or 5. They help transition chords well. In the key of G these chords are "G/B" (1/3) and "D/F#" (5/7). To hear these in action, perform a "G" (1) chord, then a "G/B" (1/3) into a "C" (4) chord. You will notice a sense of upward aural movement. The same is true of playing a "D" (5) to a "D/F#" (5/7) to a "G" (1). There will be a lifting progression happening here.

Hearing a 3m chord

As noted earlier, the 3m chord has very particular properties. While not truly a *passing chord*, it would not be a chord with which to finish a song. The 3m is very dark in tone color. Try playing a "G" (1) to a "Bm" (3m) to a "C" (4). You will hear that the middle chord, being the 3m, seems to leave the key of G. It does not technically do so, but it does catch the ear most oddly.

Hearing a ♭7 chord

A ♭7 chord is as unique to the ear as a 1 chord. You cannot miss it. The ♭7 chord is an outlier and sounds like it. In the key of G, play a "G" (1) to a "C" (4) to an "F" (♭7). Or, play a "G" (1) to a "D" (5) to an "F" (♭7). The "F" chord really stands out. The ear hears it almost as if it does not fit initially. The power in this chord is that it sounds so strange. Many bridges of songs employ this chord to add an element to the song that did not exist beforehand. Play around with the ♭7 in other keys too.

Hearing a 2-Major chord

The final chord to *hear* in this section is the 2-Major chord. You will only hear this type of chord from time to time. It is most rare, but when you hear it, *you hear it*! The 2-Major has an outlier #4 note of the major scale in it. What that means is that the ear hears a proper 2, #4 and 6, rather than the typical 2, 4 and 6 notes. This #4 note surprises the ear. In the key of G the 2-Major chord is an "A" chord. You may also hear an "A7" played. The seventh note is the tonic note, G, thus bringing a little normalcy back into the equation of such an outlier chord. Play a "G" (1) to an "A" (2-Major) to a "C" (4). Notice the lifting mechanism found in the "A" (2-Major). This can be powerful, but is typically used sparingly in pop music.

Chapter TEN:
The Awesome Use
Of The Capo

What is a capo and why is it not cheating?

When you research *capo* on dictionary.com you find that the capo is the chief of a branch of the Mafia. Wait…no. That is not the definition of capo that we are looking for. Rather, a capo is a device that when clamped or screwed down across the strings at any given fret will raise each string a corresponding number of half tones. To put this a little more applicably, a capo allows you to play what should have been barre chords using open chords. Remember, open chords tend to sound stronger than barre chords and sustain longer.

Some say that using a capo is a form of cheating. The use of the guitar capo is not a cheat in any manner. In the same way, using a guitar pick is not a cheating maneuver over using your fingers to strum your guitar. The capo is a tool that allows you to expand the abilities of your playing.

The guitar was meant to be played with as many variations of open chords as possible. An open chord assumes there is at least one string that is left untouched by any finger of the fretting hand thus allowing it to resonate openly. With any instrument, more residence produces better quality sound.

In this chapter I will devote many words to understanding some really quirky things you can do with the capo, but before we launch into that let us use the numbers we learned from the previous chapter to play in keys with open positions. Normally the key would be played using barre chord versions.

Chord Families

Key	1	2m	3m	4	5	6m	7dim	1
G	G	Am	Bm	C	D	Em	F#dim	G
G# (A♭)	G# (A♭)	A#m (B♭m)	Cm	C# (D♭)	D# (E♭)	Fm	Gdim	G# (A♭)
A	A	Bm	C#m	D	E	F#m	G#dim	A
A# (B♭)	A# (B♭)	Cm	Dm	D# (E♭)	F	Gm	Adim	A# (B♭)
B	B	C#m	D#m	E	F#	G#m	A#dim	B
C	C	Dm	Em	F	G	Am	Bdim	C
C# (D♭)	C# (D♭)	D#m (E♭m)	Fm	F# (G♭)	G# (A♭)	A#m (B♭m)	Cdim	C# (D♭)
D	D	Em	F#m	G	A	Bm	C#dim	D
D# (E♭)	D# (E♭)	Fm	Gm	G# (A♭)	A# (B♭)	Cm	Ddim	D# (E♭)
E	E	F#m	G#m	A	B	C#m	D#dim	E
F	F	Gm	Am	B♭	C	Dm	Edim	F
F# (G♭)	F# (G♭)	G#m (A♭m)	A#m (B♭m)	B	C# (D♭)	D#m (E♭m)	Fdim	F# (G♭)

This is where math comes into play. The diagram above shows every natural and sharp/flat major key and the corresponding number of chords that you will use to do some head math while transposing using your capo. If this is the first time you have ever tried to transpose music in your head please give yourself time to learn this. I use this trick every time I play guitar on stage. In fact, understanding these numbers and how they integrate with one another is the key to not needing any charts or sheet music on stage while you play. I have a friend who plays bass by understanding these numbers and has a catalog of music he has memorized that has to be well over 5000 songs. If he did not know how to do this type of chord number head math those 5000 songs would need to be written down.

First, here we are again, the 1 chord. The 1 chord is fundamental, as we have said already. In the key of G the 1 chord is "G". In the key of B the 1 chord is "B". In the key of D, the 1 chord is "D". I think you get the picture. Knowing what chord is your 1 chord will help you to derive all of the others. If you cannot hear the 1 chord then it is very hard to determine the 4, 5 and 6m chords.

Popular keys to use with the capo and why

This section details some of the most important and often used capo positions and why most guitarists use them. Please understand that there are well over a 100 ways to use the capo in a normal fashion. I cannot describe each one or you would go to sleep. I do not want that. Rather, I am outlining my favorites and the ones I use just about every guitar session.

Using the key of G, capo 4, to play in B

Capo Using the Key of G

Capo Number	1	2m	3m	4	5	6m	7dim	1
Open	G	Am	Bm	C	D	Em	F#dim	G
Capo 1	G# (A♭)	A#m (B♭m)	Cm	C# (D♭)	D# (E♭)	Fm	Gdim	G# (A♭)
Capo 2	A	Bm	C#m	D	E	F#m	G#dim	A
Capo 3	A# (B♭)	Cm	Dm	D# (E♭)	F	Gm	Adim	A# (B♭)
Capo 4	B	C#m	D#m	E	F#	G#m	A#dim	B
Capo 5	C	Dm	Em	F	G	Am	Bdim	C
Capo 6	C# (D♭)	D#m (E♭m)	Fm	F# (G♭)	G# (A♭)	A#m (B♭m)	Cdim	C# (D♭)
Capo 7	D	Em	F#m	G	A	Bm	C#dim	D
Capo 8	D# (E♭)	Fm	Gm	G# (A♭)	A# (B♭)	Cm	Ddim	D# (E♭)
Capo 9	E	F#m	G#m	A	B	C#m	D#dim	E
Capo 10	F	Gm	Am	B♭	C	Dm	Edim	F

The most popular guitar key is G. On the piano it is C. On the oboe it is "?". I haven't figured out what it is on the oboe just yet. A long time ago someone must have been dreaming that he or she could play in the key of G, but use it for the many other keys found on the guitar. The capo allows you to do just that. If you play the capo on the fourth fret and play in the key of G you are now effectively playing in the key of B. This is huge! Please note that it is best, depending on your guitar, to place your capo either exactly in the middle of the frets or on the upper third of the frets. Some guitars favor the middle, some the upper third.

I begin with the capo on the fourth fret to play in B because that is what I use it for the most. The diagram above gives you the key of G transpositions for every key up to the tenth fret. Anything higher and you should just buy a mandolin. A few of my favorites are capo on the second fret to play in the key of A, capo the fifth fret to play in C and capo the seventh fret to play in D.

Using the key of C, capo 5, to play in F

Capo Using the Key of C

Capo Number	1	2m	3m	4	5	6m	7dim	1
Open	C	Dm	Em	F	G	Am	Bdim	C
Capo 1	C# (D♭)	D#m (E♭m)	Fm	F# (G♭)	G# (A♭)	A#m (B♭m)	Cdim	C# (D♭)
Capo 2	D	Em	F#m	G	A	Bm	C#dim	D
Capo 3	D# (E♭)	Fm	Gm	G# (A♭)	A# (B♭)	Cm	Ddim	D# (E♭)
Capo 4	E	F#m	G#m	A	B	C#m	D#dim	E
Capo 5	F	Gm	Am	B♭	C	Dm	Edim	F
Capo 6	F# (G♭)	G#m (A♭m)	A#m (B♭m)	B	C# (D♭)	D#m (E♭m)	Fdim	F# (G♭)
Capo 7	G	Am	Bm	C	D	Em	F#dim	G
Capo 8	G# (A♭)	A#m (B♭m)	Cm	C# (D♭)	D# (E♭)	Fm	Gdim	G# (A♭)
Capo 9	A	Bm	C#m	D	E	F#m	G#dim	A
Capo 10	A# (B♭)	Cm	Dm	D# (E♭)	F	Gm	Adim	A# (B♭)

Place your capo across the fifth frets (again, either in middle or upper third depending on what your guitar prefers) and play in the key of C. You have effectively transposed to the key of F. My favorite way to use this is the method of playing in C described in Chapter Seven: *C and Related Chords*. Keeping that top 5 note with the pinky placed on the third fret of the first string [e] brings a beautiful consistency to each of the chords in the key of C.

Use the diagram above to play in as many keys as you would like using the key of C and your capo. Some of my favorites and ones that I use often are capo 2 in D, capo 4 in E and capo 7 in G. Playing in the key of C with a capo is also a great way to play in sharp (#) and flat (♭) keys. I especially love the sound of capo 1 in D♭ and capo 3 in E♭.

Using the key of B (thumbed version), capo 1, to play in C

Capo Using the Key of B

Capo Number	1	2m	3m	4	5	6m	7dim	1
Open	B	C#m	D#m	E	F#	G#m	A#dim	B
Capo 1	C	Dm	Em	F	G	Am	Bdim	C
Capo 2	C# (D♭)	D#m (E♭m)	Fm	F# (G♭)	G# (A♭)	A#m (B♭m)	Cdim	C# (D♭)
Capo 3	D	Em	F#m	G	A	Bm	C#dim	D
Capo 4	D# (E♭)	Fm	Gm	G# (A♭)	A# (B♭)	Cm	Ddim	D# (E♭)
Capo 5	E	F#m	G#m	A	B	C#m	D#dim	E
Capo 6	F	Gm	Am	B♭	C	Dm	Edim	F
Capo 7	F# (G♭)	G#m (A♭m)	A#m (B♭m)	B	C# (D♭)	D#m (E♭m)	Fdim	F# (G♭)
Capo 8	G	Am	Bm	C	D	Em	F#dim	G
Capo 9	G# (A♭)	A#m (B♭m)	Cm	C# (D♭)	D# (E♭)	Fm	Gdim	G# (A♭)
Capo 10	A	Bm	C#m	D	E	F#m	G#dim	A

If you have been reading this book as it is laid out then you will remember one of my favorite sections about using the thumb to play in the open key of B. Most of the time playing in the key of B means needing to use barre chords. This new way eliminates barre chords altogether. When you have mastered this positioning you can use it accompanied with your capo to play in some cool ways. If you capo the first fret and play in the key of B with the thumbed technique you are playing now in the key of C. This opens up an entirely different sound than playing in the open key of C with no capo. Try both and hear the difference. Play open "C", then "Am", then "G", then "F". Now place your capo on the first fret and try your thumbed "B" to "G#m7" to "F#sus" to "E2". That is the same progression using different fingerings and your capo. You can place the capo on the third fret to play in D. Add the capo to the fifth fret to play in E and so on.

Using the key of A, capo 2, to play in B

Capo Using the Key of A

Capo Number	1	2m	3m	4	5	6m	7dim	1
Open	A	Bm	C#m	D	E	F#m	G#dim	A
Capo 1	A# (B♭)	Cm	Dm	D# (E♭)	F	Gm	Adim	A# (B♭)
Capo 2	B	C#m	D#m	E	F#	G#m	A#dim	B
Capo 3	C	Dm	Em	F	G	Am	Bdim	C
Capo 4	C# (D♭)	D#m (E♭m)	Fm	F# (G♭)	G# (A♭)	A#m (B♭m)	Cdim	C# (D♭)
Capo 5	D	Em	F#m	G	A	Bm	C#dim	D
Capo 6	D# (E♭)	Fm	Gm	G# (A♭)	A# (B♭)	Cm	Ddim	D# (E♭)
Capo 7	E	F#m	G#m	A	B	C#m	D#dim	E
Capo 8	F	Gm	Am	B♭	C	Dm	Edim	F
Capo 9	F# (G♭)	G#m (A♭m)	A#m (B♭m)	B	C# (D♭)	D#m (E♭m)	Fdim	F# (G♭)
Capo 10	G	Am	Bm	C	D	Em	F#dim	G

The chords used on the guitar to play in the key of A are very helpful. In this key about 80% of the chords are open. This brings stability to the key and it sounds wonderful to the ear. Using the capo while playing in A allows you to use the key of A's open sound, but in keys that would normally be barre chord keys. It also allows you to use the fundamentals of A to get different results, like using the key of A, but to play in the key of C. Place your capo on the second fret. When you now play an "A" chord to an "E" chord you are actually playing a "B" to an "F#", or a 1 to a 5 chord. Depending on your song, this can be a great way to play in the key of B. This is especially true if the melody lands on the 5 note of the scale often as the key of A is built as the 5 note E at the top of the chord in several of the chords, like the "A", "E", "Bm7", "D2" and so on. Place your capo on the third fret and play in the key of A to play in the key of C. Now move it up to the fifth fret to play in the key of D.

Using the key of E, capo 2, to play in F#

Capo Using the Key of E

Capo Number	1	2m	3m	4	5	6m	7dim	1
Open	E	F#m	G#m	A	B	C#m	D#dim	E
Capo 1	F	Gm	Am	B♭	C	Dm	Edim	F
Capo 2	F# (G♭)	G#m (A♭m)	A#m (B♭m)	B	C# (D♭)	D#m (E♭m)	Fdim	F# (G♭)
Capo 3	G	Am	Bm	C	D	Em	F#dim	G
Capo 4	G# (A♭)	A#m (B♭m)	Cm	C# (D♭)	D# (E♭)	Fm	Gdim	G# (A♭)
Capo 5	A	Bm	C#m	D	E	F#m	G#dim	A
Capo 6	A# (B♭)	Cm	Dm	D# (E♭)	F	Gm	Adim	A# (B♭)
Capo 7	B	C#m	D#m	E	F#	G#m	A#dim	B
Capo 8	C	Dm	Em	F	G	Am	Bdim	C
Capo 9	C# (D♭)	D#m (E♭m)	Fm	F# (G♭)	G# (A♭)	A#m (B♭m)	Cdim	C# (D♭)
Capo 10	D	Em	F#m	G	A	Bm	C#dim	D

The guitar loves the key of E. The reason is simple and plain to hear. The key of E uses the lowest notes (in standard tuning) that the guitar allows. The key of E growls. When you add the capo to the mix you can borrow the open nature of E, but use it for some often barre chord keys, like the key of F#. Place your capo on the second fret and play in the key of E. You are playing in the key of F# when you play the chords in E, like "E", "B", "C#m" and "A2". The power of this key is that the tonic note E is at the top of most of these chords. In fact, if you use the chords from Chapter Two: "E5 and Related Chords", then the E note is at the top of each chord. Because it is the tonic or root note, there is great stability musically. Add the capo to the third fret and play in E, you are now playing in the key of G. Yes, the guitar lends itself to playing in G without a capo, but this technique broadens the types of open chords you can play. It is just another way to play the same key. Add the capo to the fifth fret to play in A. Move it up two more frets to the seventh fret to play in the key of B. Move up one more fret to the eighth fret and you are now in the key of C.

Using the key of D, capo 1, to play in E♭

Capo Using the Key of D

Capo Number	1	2m	3m	4	5	6m	7dim	1
Open	D	Em	F#m	G	A	Bm	C#dim	D
Capo 1	D# (E♭)	Fm	Gm	G# (A♭)	A# (B♭)	Cm	Ddim	D# (E♭)
Capo 2	E	F#m	G#m	A	B	C#m	D#dim	E
Capo 3	F	Gm	Am	B♭	C	Dm	Edim	F
Capo 4	F# (G♭)	G#m (A♭m)	A#m (B♭m)	B	C# (D♭)	D#m (E♭m)	Fdim	F# (G♭)
Capo 5	G	Am	Bm	C	D	Em	F#dim	G
Capo 6	G# (A♭)	A#m (B♭m)	Cm	C# (D♭)	D# (E♭)	Fm	Gdim	G# (A♭)
Capo 7	A	Bm	C#m	D	E	F#m	G#dim	A
Capo 8	A# (B♭)	Cm	Dm	D# (E♭)	F	Gm	Adim	A# (B♭)
Capo 9	B	C#m	D#m	E	F#	G#m	A#dim	B
Capo 10	C	Dm	Em	F	G	Am	Bdim	C

The second chord most guitar players learn after the chord "G" is "D". "D" is beautiful and only four strings. The power in this chord is that the third note of the scale (which is the note F# in this case) is at the top of the chord. Depending on the melody and type of the song, having the third note at the top of the chord may be the perfect sound for what you are trying to accomplish. Using the capo with the key of D positions allows you to keep that third note at the top of the chord, but playing in normally barre chord keys or open keys, but different positioning. For instance, if you apply the capo to the first fret and play in "D" you are now effectively playing in the key of E♭ (or D#, although you will never see the key of D#, it is not used). Playing a "D" to "A" to "G" with the capo on the first fret allows you to really be playing an "E♭" to "A♭" to "G♭" chords. Try each of those using barre chords and your fingers get tired and, more importantly, your chord sustain is diminished. Move your capo up one fret to the second fret and you are playing in the key of E. Move it up to fret four and you are playing in F#. Up one more fret and you are playing in the key of G. Try taking the capo off the guitar and playing in the normal, open chord version of the key of G then compare it with the capo five version using the key of D chords. These are two different ways to play in the same key. One is not better than the other. They are both options depending on the sound of music you want to make. These are inversions, like pianists use often.

Using the key of F, capo 5, to play in B♭

Capo Using the Key of F

Capo Number	1	2m	3m	4	5	6m	7dim	1
Open	F	Gm	Am	B♭	C	Dm	Edim	F
Capo 1	F# (G♭)	G#m (A♭m)	A#m (B♭m)	B	C# (D♭)	D#m (E♭m)	Fdim	F# (G♭)
Capo 2	G	Am	Bm	C	D	Em	F#dim	G
Capo 3	G# (A♭)	A#m (B♭m)	Cm	C# (D♭)	D# (E♭)	Fm	Gdim	G# (A♭)
Capo 4	A	Bm	C#m	D	E	F#m	G#dim	A
Capo 5	A# (B♭)	Cm	Dm	D# (E♭)	F	Gm	Adim	A# (B♭)
Capo 6	B	C#m	D#m	E	F#	G#m	A#dim	B
Capo 7	C	Dm	Em	F	G	Am	Bdim	C
Capo 8	C# (D♭)	D#m (E♭m)	Fm	F# (G♭)	G# (A♭)	A#m (B♭m)	Cdim	C# (D♭)
Capo 9	D	Em	F#m	G	A	Bm	C#dim	D
Capo 10	D# (E♭)	Fm	Gm	G# (A♭)	A# (B♭)	Cm	Ddim	D# (E♭)

The last key that I reference in this book is using the key of F, yes the barre chords key of F, to play in other keys. Now, the point of using the key of F and the capo is not to make your life simpler. This is why the capo is not a cheat, but rather a tool. The power in the key of F is a few of the open chords that live within. They are "C" and "Dm". I also especially like the key of F when I build the "F" chord using the thumb, as outlined in Chapter One in this book called "Barre Chords Using The Thumb". When you use the thumbed "F" then you are free to move quickly to the "C" chord and then to the "Dm". The toughest transition you encounter is to the 4 chord, which is a "B♭". I typically play a "B♭2" using the thumb, but a fully thumbed "B♭" is fine too. While this key may not be practical for everyone and for every occasion, sometimes having that open "C" and "Dm" brings about a tonal quality to the guitar that you may like. Using the key of F, the tonic note is the top note of the chord when playing "F" and then the seventh note in the scale is on top when playing a "C". If the melody also is like this, then those two chords have "married" well with the melody. For instance, if you capo the fifth fret and use the key of F then you are playing in the key of B♭. The tonic note is B♭ and the seventh note is A. If the melody moves from B♭ to A then your "F" to "C" move (remember to capo fifth fret) is a great marriage of chords/melody. You can also move the capo around to use the key of F for other keys. I like to use the key of F, capoing the first fret, to play in the key of F# (G♭). Move it up one more fret to the second fret to play in G. Yes, you can play G in open chords. Try comparing the open version of G to the capo two version. They have different qualities. Use the diagram above to walk through many of the options available to you.

Using the capo to do some stranger things

There are some really cool capo tricks that you may not know about. Just because the capo was made to go across all six strings does not mean that you have to use it that way. In this next section are some unique ideas about how to use the capo. This is not a complete list. Google and all of its power can help you find even more ideas, but this list should get you started.

One or two less string capo ideas

Using a normal, trigger type capo allows you the option of choosing to omit one or two strings. Place the capo on fret two, but from the top side of the neck, leaving open the bottom sixth string [E]. This means when you strum this open lowest string [E], which should be unaffected by the capo, all of the other strings are now capoed second fret. Play a standard "D" chord, but leave both the sixth [E] and fifth [A] strings open. Because you are capoing the second fret this effectively makes a very huge sounding "E" chord, playing in the "D" chord position. You can try "D" to "Dsus" to "D2". You are now playing gigantic sounding "E" to "Esus" to "E2" chords. Pretty awesome!

You can use two capos on one guitar and use the technique previously mentioned to play in other keys. For instance, if you add one capo across all six strings on the first fret and then a second capo on the third fret, but omitting that same sixth string [E] and play your "D" chord you have built an awesome "F" chord. Capo everything up another fret to have an "F#" chord and so on. The possibilities with this are as many as your guitar's frets will allow.

Another similar way to use the capo is to capo across the bottom five strings on the second fret, omitting the highest string [e]. This allows for a few chord options. A normal "D2" chord, but capoed up to the second fret is now a very strong sounding "E" chord. The 2 in this case has been replaced with a second tonic 1 note in this chord. If you play a "D" to an "A" to a "G" (leaving open the first string [e]) you have built three chords with the tonic E note being prominent at the top of each of those chords.

With that same capo position of the bottom five strings, now play in the key of C. Use a standard "C" chord, leaving open the top string [e]. This effectively creates a very cool "C2" chord. It is actually a "D2" chord, because we are capoed up two frets. The E note rings open throughout that new "D2" chord shape. You can move down the "C" chord scale (actually playing in the key of D) using the "C" to the "G/B" to the "Am" and so on. Leaving that top note open you have created a very neat sounding "D2", "A/C#" and "Bm11".

Using the capo in recording or on stage where one person plays capo 5 while the other has no capo, like D and open G.

The final note I will make about the capo, is that two guitar players playing at the same time, but each using different capo positions can make one massive sound. I imagine that you have attempted this before, but just in case you have not, if I capo across the seventh fret and play in the key of C and you capo across the fifth fret, but play in D we are both now playing the key of G. I hope that did not make your head spin. In fact, if we add a third guitarist and he plays in the open key of G we are performing so many key of G harmonics that everyone down the street will hear us playing. This idea is used all the time on stage and in the studio. Playing in an open key and then playing in the same key, but with a capo and different chord positions simultaneously produces a huge sound. Use the diagram below to try a few keys and capo positions together. This list is not exhaustive, but will get you started.

Multiple Capos for the Key of C

Capo Number	1	2m	3m	4	5	6m	7dim	1
Open	C	Dm	Em	F	G	Am	Bdim	C
Capo 3	A	Bm	C#m	D	E	F#m	G#dim	A
Capo 5	G	Am	Bm	C	D	Em	F#dim	G

Multiple Capos for the Key of D

Capo Number	1	2m	3m	4	5	6m	7dim	1
Open	D	Em	F#m	G	A	Bm	C#dim	D
Capo 2	C	Dm	Em	F	G	Am	Bdim	C
Capo 7	G	Am	Bm	C	D	Em	F#dim	G

Multiple Capos for the Key of E

Capo Number	1	2m	3m	4	5	6m	7dim	1
Open	E	F#m	G#m	A	B	C#m	D#dim	E
Capo 2	D	Em	F#m	G	A	Bm	C#dim	D
Capo 4	C	Dm	Em	F	G	Am	Bdim	C

Multiple Capos for the Key of G

Capo Number	1	2m	3m	4	5	6m	7dim	1
Open	G	Am	Bm	C	D	Em	F#dim	G
Capo 5	D	Em	F#m	G	A	Bm	C#dim	D
Capo 7	C	Dm	Em	F	G	Am	Bdim	C

Chapter ELEVEN: Transitioning Chords Quickly

How to transition chords well (thinking possible alternate fingers, rather than traditional)

Learning how to transition chords quickly on guitar is key to becoming a better guitar player. Transitioning means knowing your chords so well that you use as little energy as possible to move one to another. The only way to do this is to practice, practice, practice. This is head knowledge meeting physical chord positioning mechanics. You should be able to put your fretting hand into your chord positions whether you have a guitar or not. You should see them in your mind's eye. While this seems a little overkill, professional guitar players do this without any forethought.

The next few sections will help you get better at transitioning. Some of these you may do well, others you may need to work on.

The wall test

Your fingers should not move but a few millimeters off of the strings to get to the next chord. You can do a test. Stand parallel to a wall with your hand fretting a "G" chord. Your neck of your guitar should be about two inches from the wall giving you room to play your "G" chord, but not much else. Now transition to a "D" chord. If you hit the wall so hard during that transition that your hand now hurts then your fingers are flying too far off the guitar to make an efficient transition. In essence you are wasting valuable transition time because your fingers are moving further off the guitar than they need to be. The exact amount of space required to be as efficient as possible is really up to you. You want to be able to transition between chords seamlessly. If you are having any downtime transitioning chords then there is something more to be developed with your mechanics.

Inefficient guitar playing

The worst thing you can do to transition is to take a finger off the guitar only to put it back where it just came from. For instance, if I am playing a "G" chord where my ring finger (3) is on the third fret of the second string [B] and I transition to a "D" chord, that ring finger does not need to move. Beginner guitarists make this mistake often. Instead of allowing that finger to come off of the guitar, use it to your advantage. Make your ring finger (3) become the pivot point allowing your other fingers to fall in place because that ring finger was already there. This works for a myriad of chords. Another example is "G" to "Cadd9" to "Dsus" to "Em7". All four of those chords keep the third frets of the second [B] and first [e] strings pressed down by the ring (3) and pinky (4) fingers, respectively. While this may seem obvious, if you move those last two fingers for any reason while transitioning between those chords you have lost precious pace. The examples I have used are very simple, but the principle needs to be used with every chord transition that has the opportunity to have a pivot point.

Always be thinking one or two chords ahead, not in the moment`

The next transition topic that will put you light years beyond the next guitarist is to always be thinking one to two chords ahead of what you are currently playing. You may also want to think in terms of measures ahead depending on the type of music. This is how the chess champion wins every time. They always think two and three moves ahead. One of the worst things that musicians can do is to be playing only in the moment. The best musicians are always thinking ahead. Much like when you drive, if you are not consistently watching the cars one and two ahead, you may end up meeting them unexpectedly in a car crash. It is this clairvoyance that allows you to stay safe and to switch lanes when you see the car ahead of you is a minivan with a mom and dad in an argument. In order to think ahead you have to employ two things.

- You have to know the song you are playing. Knowing a song means that you have spent more than thirty seconds pouring over a quick lead sheet. You have to internalize the chord structure of what the writer intended. The key of the song has to be firmly rooted in your mind.
- The other part of thinking ahead is using your head math that was described in a previous chapter. As you develop being able to *hear* in

numbers, you also will be able to anticipate what chord is next because your ear will sense it. For instance, if you are on a 1 chord, your ear will be assuming you will probably be headed toward a 4, 5 or 6m. Those are typical chords to transition to from a 1. Using head math is a critical component to being able to think ahead.

Alternate fingering positions of fundamental chords.

The final way that I outline in this book to be better at transitioning chords is to learn to play all of your fundamental chords using multiple fingering options. In other words, you can play an "A2" chord with your index (1) and middle (2) fingers. However, you can also do so with your middle finger (2) and your ring finger (3). Also, you could do the same with your ring (3) and pinky (4) fingers. Depending on which chord you are heading to next will best dictate which fingering position for your chord you will want to use. For example, I almost always play an "Esus" chord using my middle (2), ring (3) and pinky (4) fingers on the second frets of the fifth [A], fourth [D] and third [G] strings. This allows me to transition to "E" by simply removing my pinky finger (4) revealing my index finger (1) already in place on the first fret of the third string [G]. Traditionally the "Esus" is taught using fingers (1), (2) and (3). In using that position you would need to move every finger off the guitar to get to an "E" chord. That wastes time.

Do your best to learn as many practical ways to play some of the most fundamental chords as you know how. This may mean convincing your mind that sometimes playing the barre chord "G" or thumbed barre chord "G" is a quicker transition chord from the "F" chord than playing the traditional "G". The point being that every chord has at least one alternate way to finger it or a different chord version that may a more suitable chord to transition to. If a chord seems too tough for you, practice that chord until it becomes second nature. You always want to be growing and progressing as a guitar player.

Chapter TWELVE: The Amazing Guitar Pick

The guitar pick

The guitar pick, or plectrum if you are in Great Britain, is about as important as the guitar strings are today. Said to be thousands of years old, the guitar pick is a device used to strum or pick guitar strings rather than our raw fingers. Most of us are used to playing with picks made of hard, durable plastic, but other materials can provide some nifty tones, as we will discuss.

Light, medium and heavy

Picks come in three basic weights, with the option to be slightly thinner or thicker than the others to form varying degrees of each. Normally you will purchase guitar picks in light, medium and heavy gauges. Light picks are typically around .5mm, medium .75mm and heavy averaging .9mm. Extra light and extra heavy exist as well. Extra light guitar picks are like strumming your guitar with a feather while extra heavy are like using your car door. Preference is key here. I typically use a medium pick. Most of my cohorts use lights. This section identifies different tones with each.

Light picks are by their very nature thinner than all of the others. Thus they tend to *give* more when being played. I typically use light picks when I want the sound of my guitar to have an airy sense. Because the pick will not strike as heavy, the sound is not as loud. There is less *attack*, which is the initial striking sound that the pick makes.

Medium picks will sound a little louder than lights and have a stronger attack as well. The downside is that they do not *give* as much and some players find them harder to use. I recommend getting picks of all sizes, shapes and materials and entertaining each of these options.

Heavy picks are by their very nature made of very tough, thick materials. Typically bass players who use a pick will utilize these heavier picks. I have never used heavy picks to play in my day to day strumming, however I have used them for recording. Heavy picks provide very strong attack. In certain cases they are perfect.

Pick material types

Guitar picks come in more and more materials everyday. The two basic materials that you will find *in the wild* are: acrylic (hard plastic) and nylon (softer plastic). Acrylic picks, like those used in V-Picks, are extremely durable and can be transparent. The toughness of these picks allows them to strike the string stronger than other types of picks. This alters the sound by making the attack stronger and overall sound level louder. Nylon picks are typically softer and thus deliver a softer sound. Typically acrylic picks will keep their shape, while nylon picks will bend and break over a period of months. Guitar picks are so cheap today that it is best to keep a small bag of them in your guitar gig bag.

Plastic is not the only material that can be used for guitar picks. You can use just about anything you would like to strike the strings. I have owned wooden picks and have seen glass picks. While I have never tried a metal pick, I would like to. Do your best to experiment with as many pick sizes, shapes and materials as you are able. While you may select your specific brand and size, be flexible and make sure you have options in your bag for that unique-sound occasion.

Ways to hold a pick

Different ways of holding a guitar pick will alter the tone after striking. Typically I use my thumb on one side of the guitar pick and then my index and middle finger on the other side. This provides a lot of grip and strength. However, if I want a softer tone I will release the middle finger and only use my thumb and index finger. I can then strike the string a little softer, allowing fewer overtones to develop. This gives a unique characteristic to the sound.

I have friends who will keep their thumb closer to the strings, allowing them to deaden strings a small amount strum to strum. This technique offers a totally unique sound as well.

While holding your pick your unused fingers may be kept as a tight fist or your may prefer the method of letting your fingers remain straightened. That method looks a bit like you are wringing your hands out after washing them in the sink. I prefer the closed method because I saw Noel Gallagher (of the band Oasis) doing this some years ago. As far as I can tell both methods are acceptable. If one works better for you, sweet!

MICAH BROOKS

Chapter THIRTEEN: Alternate Guitar Tunings

Alternate tunings are used today and not just the past

In the mid 90's, alternate tunings were all the rage. Every band, like the Goo Goo Dolls and Creed used them. Today, you hear of alternate tunings less and less. However, I believe they are still useful and may find a come back.

An alternate tuning is just that: an alternate way to tune one or more of your guitar strings from normal standard tuning to create a different sound with the guitar. There are literally, not figuratively, hundreds of ways to alternatively tune your guitar. I will outline a few, but my hope in this chapter is that you will explore the art and science behind the alternate tuning and not just the few examples that I give and will explore even more.

Alternate tunings are used for a few reasons. One is that they can make playing open chords easier and keep a certain set of open notes resounding through every chord without much heavy chord transitioning. The other is that they can be used to play in lower or higher keys without the use of a capo.

Tuning a few strings down or up

No one says that you *have to* tune to E, A, D, G, B, e. That is standard tuning, but it is not required. Depending on the type of music or what kind of guitar you are playing, some of the following tunings may be just the type of tuning you need to play that kind of guitar or genre. These next few tunings alter some of the strings from normal into less traditional tuning.

Dropped D

Dropped D tuning is used by heavy metal guitar players daily. The lowest string [E] is dropped a whole step to a D note. You tune that string down from the E note until you see a D note on your tuner. This allows the bottom three strings [E] (Now a D), [A] and [D] to be played open together to form a very growly "D5" chord. On a distorted electric guitar this power chord "D5" is extremely dark and used in that manner a lot. This is not to say that playing in Dropped D means that you have to be a heavy metal guitarist. I bring it up solely because that style of music employs this trick often. Acoustic guitars can be tuned down to Dropped D for a neat, growly sound as well. This one is fun with which to experiment. I recommend Googling ways to play in Dropped D and songs that employ it.

DADGAD

DADGAD, said aloud it sounds like: "Dad - Gad", is a way of tuning several strings down to create a very neat open sounding tuning. To get to DADGAD you must tune your sixth [E] string down to a D note by one whole step. Then you lower your second string [B] down one whole step to an A. Last, you lower your first string [e] to a D note, again by one whole step. When you place your index finger on the second fret of the fourth string [G], making it now an A note, and strum all six strings you produce a beautiful and open sounding chord. This is the power of DADGAD.

DADF#AD

DADF#AD is not as widely used, but I love it more than DADGAD. In DADF#AD you tune everything down as you have in DADGAD, but you also lower your third string [G] down one half step to an F#. This allows you to play like you would with the DADGAD tuning, but you do not need to touch any strings to produce an open sounding chord. Strum across all six strings to hear a beautiful and rich "D" chord. If you place your index finger on the fifth fret of the lowest string [E] (now tuned down to a D) and strum all six strings, muting the fifth string [A] with your index finger, you have formed a "G" chord. Move it up to the seventh fret and you have an "A" chord. This tuning is fun with which to experiment.

Tuning the high string [e] down to a D note

This tuning does not have a catchy name and it is not all that useful, but here it is anyway. Much like when using a capo across only the bottom five strings and leaving the first string [e] open, you can tune the first string [e] down to a D note (one whole step) to create an alternate tuning. This may be a helpful tuning when you are playing in the key of D to keep that newly dropped D note in most of the chords as an open first string. Another fun way to play this is to play a standard "C" chord, but now with that open D note in play it creates a beautiful "C2" chord.

Tuning everything down or up.

This section is dedicated to tuning your entire set of guitar strings up or down, much like you would with a capo, but this time you are using your tuning pegs to do the work.

Half step down

You can tune each string down one half step to create a new sound. This means what once were your normal strings as E, A, D, G, B, e are now E♭, A♭, D♭, G♭, B♭, e♭. The beauty of this tuning is two fold. One, you can now play a "G" chord and you are effectively playing a G♭ (F#) chord. This technique is much like having a capo that allows you to detune a half step. The other benefit is that because this is an alternate tuning, our ears are not accustomed to hearing it played. The freshness of this tuning often catches our attention.

Whole step down (fret buzz...)

I keep my acoustic guitar tuned an entire whole step down, not just a half step down like in the previous section. In doing so, I am able to use my standard "G" shape chord, but to play an "F" chord. I am able to play in the key of F, but rather than playing "F", "B♭" and "C" shapes, I am able to play "G", "C" and "D" shapes. As we have spoken before, a guitar loves open chords. There is so much more resonance. Much like playing one half step down, playing an entire step down is very unusual to the ear. In fact, I get asked a lot if I am playing in open tunings because playing a whole step down has a DADGAD-like quality to it. The down side to this tuning though is that your guitar strings were not made to be this loose on the neck. Depending on your guitar, there may be too much fret buzz happening from the looseness of the strings. You can either have the neck adjusted to suit the lower rumbling or you may be able to use thicker strings to accommodate the tension needed to work best with your guitar. Experiment to find what works best with you.

Half step up

This next section may at first appear strange. There are times when guitarists will tune all of their guitar strings up. This may be by a half step or more. You may be thinking: why not use a capo? It is true, you will essentially be accomplishing the same thing as a capo, but with one mighty difference. Your guitar was made to work by using the nut of your guitar. This connection causes the most resonance. Most capos have a small, but audible dampening effect. When I capo fret one and record my guitar as opposed to tuning the entire instrument up one half step I will notice slightly less resonance. This is very nit picky but when it comes to recording this obsessive nature can be a critical component to success. The other benefit is that you are able to get the tuning of those open notes just right. When using a capo, the capo can move, bringing you slightly above or below pitch depending on the strength of the capo. I will say, I only tune up one or maybe two half tones. Anything beyond that may cause too much tension on the neck of your guitar or the strings may even break.

Nashville Tuning

One of the coolest tunings ever created has to be the Nashville tuning, also known as high strung tuning. In this tuning the lowest four strings, E, A, D and G are replaced with lighter gauge strings to allow those notes to be tuned up an exact octave from where they previously were. Technically, this is still a standard tuning, but if you ever string a guitar this way, you will hear a very beautiful and high sound representation of the standard tuning. Pink Floyd, The Rolling Stones, Matchbox Twenty, Kansas and many more famous artists use this tuning from time to time while recording. It delivers a different flair to their music. If you are familiar with a twelve string guitar, this is a similar sound.

Removing a string on purpose

The final alternate tuning we should discuss is not really a tuning at all, but rather the removal of an unwanted note or string. For example, I can remove my second [B] string completely from the guitar while playing in the key of E to get rid of the B note entirely from all open chords played. I might remove my fifth string [A] when playing in the key of G so I do not have to be concerned about muting it as much, like I normally do playing that key. This type of tuning would not be practical on stage, but in the studio this is common.

Some guitarists in the studio will place a washcloth taped around the first and second frets to dampen any string that is not being played while performing a high neck solo. This makes sure that there are not any unwanted open notes being played during that important guitar solo. Because your fretting hand is high up the neck, the washcloth does not dampen any note that you are intending to play. It only gets rid of unwanted open string notes. Pretty awesome!

Chapter FOURTEEN: How To Notate Guitar Music

Normal notation

Plain and simply put, you should learn how to read sheet music. However, this chapter does not teach how to do that. Ha! There are children's books all the way to entire collegiate textbooks that can teach you how to read standard music notation. This is also called sheet music or lead sheets. I believe that every guitar player should be familiar with how to read music just as much as any pianist should. You ought to know what a quarter note is and that four of them together equal the same duration a whole note. A half note is held for two beats while the eighth note is worth an eighth beat of a standard 4|4 measure. If you are completely lost, I recommend beginning your learning by Googling "music notation for beginners".

Guitar Tabs

There is an alternative type of sheet music that has been derived from standard music notation, but easier for guitarists to read. This is called guitar tablature or guitar tabs. It also helps that Microsoft Word is the primary way of creating these documents, rather than music notation software, like Finale or Sibelius (although they each can create guitar tabs).

Guitar tabs use six lines that correspond to the usual six strings on your guitar (sheet music uses the standard five lines). Numbers are then placed along certain strings and at certain times to indicate what fret is to be fingered and when. Guitar tabs can be the quickest and easiest way to learn a guitar line or write out the chords for a song. There are two very important disadvantages to using guitar tablature when trying to communicate a musical idea. One is that guitar tabs, especially those made for the internet through Microsoft Word, do not contain measures or note durations. This makes it incredibly hard to know where a chord or note transitions or how long to hold it. The other downside is that you do not know which finger to use to fret the number being displayed. All you know is that the fret number needs to be pressed down. Standard music notation would not offer this information either.

Shorthand chord writing

Sometimes writing out a chord for someone is not worth drawing an entire diagram with six strings, several frets, which finger number to use, etc. With the invention of the internet came the chord shorthand. Now, you can write out the standard "G" chord like this: 320033. The first number is the lowest [E] string and the last number is the highest [e] string. You indicate an open string with a "0" and a string that you do not play with an "x". For instance, a "G5" chord, where you mute the fifth string [A] is written as 3x0033. A standard "A" chord would be x02220. The more familiar you are with this type of shorthand the more these numbers look like the actual chord to you. I have included a list of several shorthand chords below.

List of shorthand chords

"G"   320033
"A"   x02220
"B"   x24442
"C"   x32010
"D"   xx0232
"E"   022100
"F"   133211
"Am"   x02210
"Bm"   x24432
"Dm"   xx0231
"Em"   022000

Chapter FIFTEEN: How To Play Rhythm Guitar In A Band

The down strum is king

One of the most important keys to playing rhythm in a band (especially if you are playing acoustic guitar) is to know that *the down strum is king*. This is a concept I learned early on, but seems almost like a professional secret these days. Up strums are for accents almost exclusively. The down strum should be used for most downbeats. This is especially true of beats 1 and 3. Depending on the type of music you may also want to use down strums for beats 2 and 4. Using up strums for accents means that you use them sparingly.

The reason the down strum is king is that every down strum begins with the lower notes of the guitar. In most cases the first note being strummed is the tonic or root note of the chord. This stabilizes the chord. On the other hand, up strums play the root note last. The stability is lost to the ear. I typically play 10:1 down strums to those that are up strums.

The kick drum sets that beat for everyone else

When you play in a band each instrument has a responsibility in the greater mix. The kick drum may be the most foundational and important instrument on stage. In an orchestra this may be the conductor and the timpani, but in pop music, the kick drum sets the defined beat. This is why I would rather have a strong drummer who keeps excellent time more than two fancy electric guitar players and a bass player who can play 64th notes. A good drummer can cover the sins of a mediocre bass player. The kick drum defines whether the band will play very straight, like on beats 1, 2, 3 and 4 or if the entire groove should be syncopated, as in adding some up beats, like the "and" of 2. For instance, the groove may be straight like the kick drum on 1 and 3 with the snare drum on beats 2 and 4. A syncopated example would be the kick drum on 1 and the "and" of 2 rather than the "3" with the snare on 2 and 4. While the measure is still a 4|4 measure, the band has a feel like it has been thrust forward a half a beat. This is all due to the kick drum taking control of the beat and the band following suit.

The 100% Rule

Why is a pie round? Why not square, star shaped or oval? The traditional pie is round because it promotes even cooking throughout. So, why pie? Micah, why are you talking about pies? One of the most common examples teachers use to explain percentage is through the delicious treat, pie. If I give you a $1/4^{th}$ of a pie (or 25%) then I am left with $3/4^{th}$ (75%). No more, no less. 100% of the total pie is made up of its individual slices.

The 100% rule when playing in a band, whether as a singer or musician, is the principle that your band is made up of the sum of its parts. The unit creates 100% of the total music coming from the speakers. Great bands make sure that each piece is contributing their percentage at the perfect rate to help make up the entire 100%. For example, drums and vocals are usually the loudest parts of any band mix. If the drummer realizes he needs to only play a 30% role in the mix he may be more careful in how loud he plays or how often. Similarly, a vocalist may need to be busier or louder in order to carry her 40%. After the drums and vocalists have eaten their part of the pie there is only 30% sonic space available for the guitarists, bassists and keyboardists. They may have to play more spacey, simpler or be more aware of those performing around them.

Sometimes bands get the meaning of the 100% rule, 100% wrong. Band members think that if they are on-stage they should play 100% of the time. It is just not true! If everyone plays all the time, and you have a 5 piece band, then you have really made 500% total output. You would be overwhelming your sound system and your audience.

Better bands and teams realize the need for sonic space. If the bass, drums and vocalists are utilizing 70-80% of that space then I, as a guitar player, should be careful to not take up more than the remaining 20%. I would play in spots where others are not playing and overall, I need to play less.

When you employ additional musicians, like percussion, strings or brass, it is important to give attention to their sonic space requirements and perform accordingly.

Whenever you hear and see a really good band performing at 100% output, usually the sound is very enjoyable and engaging. You can easily hear the vocalists' diction. You can distinguish between guitar one and guitar two. I would imagine this great band or worship team has intentionally worked together to play as one team or blend as one voice.

Many times vocalist blend is another form of the 100% rule. The lead vocal takes precedence to the background vocals. Those performing BGVs should be aware of each other as to form a tight knit group. If one voice overpowers the rest it is obvious to its hearers and ruins the mix.

When a team performs at peak 100%, the sound person is often making very few tweaks to their mix. The band or worship team mixes themselves, so to speak. When a team is way off balance then the sound man's job is very busy and stressful.

I challenge you to think of your role in your organization. Should you be playing more? Less? If you are not the lead musician, could you still influence your team to operate within the 100% rule?

The acoustic plays more when the song is light; less when heavy. Use the down strum diamond to cut through mix.

The final note about playing rhythm guitar is especially for acoustic guitarists. The acoustic guitar can either be a tunable hi hat (meaning hashy and indistinguishable in the mix) or the best use of the right combination of tone and percussive nature coming from any instrument on stage. A tunable hi hat is an acoustic guitar player who paints fences. They strum their guitar up and down, up and down, over and over. On the other hand, a strong rhythm acoustic guitarist will ebb and flow. They will use down strums to their advantage, while minimizing up strums for only critical moments when accents make sense. As a general rule, playing down strums on beats 1, 2, 3 an 4 will fit well into most songs and mixes. This is especially true of beats 1 and 3.

As a general rule, the acoustic guitar carries the same responsibility as the keyboard/pad in a mix. Meaning that when the band is dynamically light, the acoustic guitar can be busier. You may want to play more intricate strumming patterns. When the band is more full, like in later choruses and huge bridges the acoustic guitar may want to restrain to playing diamonds (whole notes) or stop playing all together. Timely used diamonds will often cut through the mix of a huge chorus more than a lot of strumming will. This is a *less is more* technique. This lets the instrument mean more when it is playing during the quieter moments. The idea is that you play more of a percentage of the pie when called upon, but diminish when other instruments take more prominence. This is what professionals do. So can you!

Final Greetings

Yahoo! You are at the end of the course! If you read every page and implemented over 100 new chords and strategies, way to go! Now, the best thing you can do with this material is to share it with others. While I would love for them to buy this book, this is not what I mean. Possibly the best way for you to sharpen your skills is to teach another guitarist what you have learned. Find someone who is primed for this material and see if you can teach them your new high "Eadd9" chord. Try walking a newer guitarist or any type of musician through learning head music and basic music theory. The old saying *those who can't, teach* is about as dumb as saying that chocolate is not tasty. Teaching someone a skill, like playing some of these chords, is one of the best ways for you to solidify your learning.

The other point I will make is that learning these chords and then sitting at home with them is not enough. Do your best to find at least one more musician and play together. John Lennon met Paul McCartney because Paul new more chords than John. The two strengthened one another. You and I need one another. I personally recommend trying to find someone in your local church with whom you can perform. Your local church may also have positions open on their worship and music teams. Get in contact with some of the main leaders you see on stage. Let them know you are interested. I know at my church if someone presents themselves in this way we have an audition process in place for us to get to know them. It is important that you play with other musicians if you are not.

I want to hear from you! Seriously, email me at: micah@micahbrooks.com. Let's talk about what you learned. If you have questions or need anything clarified I want to help. Visit micahbrooks.com for more ways to connect.

Blessing!

"I pray that the many strange, but cool chords that this learner has applied will broaden their use of their guitar. I thank you that you created music theory to be guideposts for how to play. As they move forward with their craft, I pray that you continue to add to their learning. Bless and watch over them and may their guitar playing days be many. In Jesus' name, amen."

In This Series and Additional Resources

Find out about the other books in this series and sign up for the Micah Brooks "Stay Connected" mailing list.

This is book three in the Micah Brooks Guitar Authority Series books. The first book, *Worship Guitar In Six Weeks,* is a six week course designed to bring a guitar player from knowing little about guitar onto the stage in six weeks. The second book is *42 Guitar Chords Everyone Should Know*. *Guitar Secrets Revealed* is intended to be for intermediate to experienced guitar players. If you know a beginner guitarist, please recommend these previous books to them. Now that you have finished *Guitar Secrets Revealed*, let's make sure we stay connected.

Find out about the Micah Brooks Guitar Authority Series books and more at:

www.micahbrooks.com

Email Micah

Email Micah Brooks at micah@micahbrooks.com. I want to know who you are. I have a heart to meet people. It is my privilege to respond to my emails personally. Please feel free to connect with me. I will glad to answer questions or set up a Skype call as you need.

Join the Micah Brooks "Stay Connected" mailing list to stay up to date

Subscribe to the Micah Brooks Ministry "Stay Connected" mailing list and stay current with my latest book releases. My email list is always free and intended to deliver high value content to your inbox. I do not sell your email address to someone else. I simply want to be able to stay connected with you. Click here to join.

www.micahbrooks.com/join

Reviews on Amazon

Reviews are the lifeblood of authors. If you are willing to leave feedback, I would be humbled and grateful. Please do so at:

www.amazon.com

Skype Lessons

I would be glad to consider giving you online guitar lessons. If you would like to apply for lessons with Micah Brooks via Skype visit my website to find out more. I cannot accept every student, but I would be happy to hear your story and see what you would like to accomplish.

www.micahbrooks.com

Join The Christian Guitar Community Facebook Group

All readers of this book are welcome to join The Christian Guitar Community Facebook group. Meet guitar players from around the world. You may post your insights about learning guitar. You are welcome to ask questions and comment on other posts. The group is designed to be a community. We ask everyone in the group to interact, which makes the content fun and engaging.

www.facebook.com/groups/thechristianguitarcommunity

More About Micah Brooks Ministry

For more about Micah Brooks and my ministry, including books, CDs, mp3s, clothing and art designs, online store, blogs, devotions, speaking and performing dates please go to:

www.micahbrooks.com

Follow Micah Brooks

Everyone is welcome to follow Micah Brooks on these social media platforms:

Facebook: @micahbrookspage
www.facebook.com/micahbrookspage

Twitter: @mchbrks
www.twitter.com/mchbrks

LinkedIn: Micah Brooks
www.linkedin.com/in/micahbrooks

Instagram: @mchbrks
www.instagram.com/mchbrks

If you have trouble connecting to any of these social media accounts, please visit www.micahbrooks.com.

Micah is Editor In Chief at www.worshippublishing.com, www.uprightpassiveincome.com and www.songwritingcreative.com

Worship Publishing is a resource website that includes books, daily devotions, music, podcasts, product reviews and many more recommendations. Use our wealth of staff writers and high quality guest post content to better your walk with the Lord. Visit: www.worshippublishing.com

Upright Passive Income is a company devoted to helping entrepreneurs achieve their vision and dreams. Everyone should have a side business of some kind and earning passive income is an awesome way to do so. Great examples include self-publishing a book, affiliate marketing and video marketing. Visit: www.uprightpassiveincome.com to learn about all of our high quality services.

Songwriting Creative is a website devoted to songwriting in all forms. From beginner writers to the most advanced, we each still have room to grow and expand our skills and craft. SongwritingCreative.com is intended to be a songwriting community and we do our best to facilitate. Check it out.

Appendix

- 1. How to buy a guitar without taking a bath
- 2. How to change guitar strings with a secret locking technique

1. How to buy a guitar. A quick and easy guide to the things you have to know before you head to a guitar store!

"Friends never let friends go into a guitar store alone." [End Tweet]

Here's how to buy a guitar! IMPORTANT: Never go into a guitar store to buy a guitar without facts about the price and availability of that guitar in your area. Most music store salesmen are about as motivated as used car salesmen. They know which guitars have the highest margin. If you go into your store without a plan you may come out with your salesman's favorite pick, but what may not be the best guitar for you in the long run. My recommendation is that you take an experienced guitar player whom you trust with you.

A note about price range

I am often asked "What guitar should I get?". My answer is always the same: "What's your price range?". Acoustic guitars in particular live in specific price bands. The entry level acoustic usually ranges: $100-$300. The intermediate: $500-$1,000. And the professional: $1,000 and up. I intentionally left out the $300-$500 range. The biggest difference between an entry level and an intermediate guitar is the type of wood and binding that the luthier, or guitar maker, uses to create the instrument. You will discover better instruments as you cross the $500 barrier. Normally you will not notice a significant difference between a guitar for $250 and one for $400. I recommend beginner guitarists purchase in the $250-$300 range. You may find an acoustic guitar for $299 and then the same guitar for $449, but with electronics (making it an acoustic electric guitar). Do not be fooled into paying that extra $150 for electronics that cost the manufacturer $8 to install. The majority of their cost is in drilling the holes in the wood. Rather, buy the nicest $299 acoustic guitar you can find and then add the electronics later. You will be glad you did. The sound quality when plugged in will be much better. When you begin to look at intermediate or professional guitars is the time when you may want to consider an onboard pickup and electronics package that comes pre-installed. Most of the time those pickups are hand selected for that particular instrument and are a part of the guitar's original design.

Ask for a bundle

While you are negotiating the final price for your guitar, consider asking for a few items as part of a bundle. You will want a new set of strings. You do not know how long your guitar has been on the shelf, being played by possibly hundreds of people. You will also need a strap (get one you like), a tuner (if you have a smart phone you could download an app) and a capo.

Spring for the case

Finally, spring for the hardshell case that is made for your guitar. Unlike a grand piano that moves once a decade, your guitar is small enough to go places. It will be in your SUV trunk with all your baseball gear. Maybe your little sister will have to sit on it in the middle row of your parent's minivan. Who knows? Get the case that fits your guitar snugly so that it is best protected when you are not performing or practicing.

Go in with a plan. Do your homework!

To sum up, go to your music store with a plan (and with a musician friend) and be prepared to negotiate for a bundled price. Also, remember to budget for a hardshell case if you are able. Some stores may want to sell you a warranty. While I am sure it seems tempting, typically warranties have deductibles and are not worth all they are said to be worth. If you are buying a lower end instrument (especially if this is your first), know that you are going to get scratches, bumps and bruises on it. In my opinion, you may want to disregard the store's warranty pitch. That's it! Happy buying!

2. Choosing the right guitar strings

Guitar strings are the lifeblood of a guitar. They are normally made of hard metal and come in various thicknesses. You'll notice that they are around 3-4 feet long and have a small ball on the end of each string. You can purchase them with or without coating. Coating is a protective layer of material laid over the metal on the string and is said to increase string life. As you touch your strings your fingers leave acid residue which builds up over time. That residue causes the strings to become dull. You can actually feel the string itself and tell that it has built up too much residue. That means it's time to change strings. Depending on how often you play, that could mean you need to change your strings as often as each month or as little as every six months. I recommend not letting your strings go longer than six months.

I recommend purchasing a set of *light* strings. That means that the thickness of each string will be in what is considered the guitar string *light* class. Typically that means your highest string 1 [e] will have a gauge of .10 - .12 mm. *Light* strings are easier to push down on the fretboard than medium strings, but not as easy as super light strings.

While there may seem to be about 100 brands and styles, simply choose a package or two of strings that meet your budget. A normal package of professional, non-coated acoustic guitar strings should cost around $6. Coated strings, which may last longer, should cost $10-$13. I use coated strings because I play so often. For your first few sets of strings, you may consider buying regular strings and then upgrading as you get better; especially as you play more often.

How to change strings

Changing your own guitar strings is a skill you should acquire. Yes, the store where you buy your strings will put them on for you, but they usually charge for that. Plus, when you change your own strings, you get to confirm that there are not any new chips or dings in the body. You identify any problems that have arisen. Also, you get to clean your guitar. The shop is not gong to take near as much care for your instrument as you will.

To replace old strings with new ones, I typically use the following method and order. You can attempt other methods, but this is what some other professionals and I do.

First, remove the old strings. Do this by loosening the tuning pegs to the point where the string you want released can be pulled out of its hole. I like to loosen all six strings from the headstock before removing them from the body. Once all strings are off, throw them away. They are old, used and not worth keeping. Not even as spares. Most music stores sell individual new strings, if you feel like you want to have some as spares. Old strings are stretched out and often covered in finger residue. They are spent.

Next, I clean the guitar and neck. I use guitar cleaner or polish for the body, back of neck and headstock, but not the fretboard. Make sure you get all finger prints and any unwanted residue off your guitar. For the fretboard, I use a guitar-specific lemon oil. It refreshes the wood of the neck while still cleaning your frets. Lastly, and this is only for instruments with a sound hole (like an acoustic guitar), I take compressed spray air (often used to clean electronics) and spray out any dust in the chamber of the body. When dust settles inside the body it causes sound to vibrate in a different way than the guitar was designed to thus changing or dampening its tone.

After you have sufficiently cleaned your guitar, you can move forward in putting on your new strings. I recommend beginning with the thickest string [E]. Most acoustic guitars have a tooth-like pin that needs to be pushed back in after you have inserted the ball bottom of the new string. Once in place you should be able to stretch the string the entire length of the guitar and neck. Put the end of the string into the first hole on the left side of the tuner area on the headstock. I recommend making sure that as you begin turning the tuning peg the string be wound so that it moves the end of the string toward the middle of the headstock. This is rather than having the string wind toward the outside of the guitar. In other words, for the sixth, fifth and fourth string, the strings should wind counterclockwise and the third, second, and first should wind clockwise. If all tuning pegs are on one side I still recommend winding to the center of the neck.

A secret locking string technique

A secret that I learned a long time ago about how to wind your strings so that they tightly hold and stay in tune is to let the end of the wound string first go UNDER the string being tuned. After the string has been under once, make the remaining turns go OVER the string being tuned. It creates a type of locking mechanism.

Repeat the steps above for all remaining strings. You should now have all new strings on your guitar. Congratulations!

You will need to do a few final steps before you are ready to tune up. First, you will need to stretch out your new strings. This gets any leftover loose slack out at the strings at the headstock. It also lets the strings themselves begin to balance. They came from the factory pretty rigid. To stretch your strings, begin by pulling them off the guitar neck about 2-3 inches. Be safe! You want to stretch them at three second intervals for three to fives sets, releasing the string in between. After you have sufficiently stretched your strings it will be time to cut the ends of the strings that are still hanging on at the headstock. Make sure you are cutting off the string excess and not the actual string that is new and now attached to the guitar. I have made that mistake before and it's not fun! Finally, use needle nose pliers to bend the tiny ends of the strings down and into the headstock. Your goal should be to not have any dangerous metal sticking outward toward you to make you bleed if you were to touch that area. I always keep a Band-Aid in my guitar string changing kit. Ha!

About The Author

My name is Micah Brooks and I am a worship pastor, author and songwriter from Nashville, Tennessee, USA. My passion is to see Jesus' people lift up and worship Jesus' name.

While playing music is part of my profession, I am a family man in life. I am married to wife Rochelle. Together we have three children (as of 2016, we may have more by now, ha!): Liam, Aisley and Jovie. We attend World Outreach Church where I am a worship pastor. The whole family enjoys running in the Tennessee heat, and I also enjoy playing church league softball.

Micah has been a guitar teacher and coach for over ten years. Most people learn best by having one-on-one instruction. This book and the others in this series, such as *Worship Guitar In Six Weeks* and *42 Guitar Chords Everyone Should Know*, were created with the student in mind. They are each the best of the lessons that a guitar student will receive from Micah. The guitar is one of the greatest tools for modern worship. When the guitar is used to expand God's kingdom, the opportunities are endless. All glory to Jesus Christ!

You can find out more about Micah Brooks including my other books, music, videos, websites and resources at www.micahbrooks.com.

Made in the USA
Columbia, SC
17 July 2025